John Dawson Ross

Burns' Clarinda

Brief Papers Concerning the Poet's Renowned Correspondent

John Dawson Ross

Burns' Clarinda
Brief Papers Concerning the Poet's Renowned Correspondent

ISBN/EAN: 9783337777807

Printed in Europe, USA, Canada, Australia, Japan

Cover: Foto ©Thomas Meinert / pixelio.de

More available books at **www.hansebooks.com**

BURNS' CLARINDA:

Brief Papers concerning the Poet's Renowned Correspondent.

COMPILED FROM VARIOUS SOURCES BY

JOHN D. ROSS, LL.D.,

Author of "Scottish Poets in America," "Random Sketches on Scottish Subjects,"
"A Cluster of Poets," and Editor of "Celebrated Songs of Scotland,"
"Round Burns's Grave," "Highland Mary," "All About
Burns," "The Burns Scrap Book," "Centenary
Burnsiana," "Burnsiana," etc. etc.

"It is no idle dream
That we have heard a voice from Heaven:
'Behold this heart hath lovèd much,
And much to it shall be forgiven.'"
—AGNES MAULE MACHER.

New York:
THE RAEBURN BOOK COMPANY,
1897.

" NOUGHT can ever be unwelcome to Scottish readers which comes so near to the heart of ROBERT BURNS as to treat of one whose grace and beauty and intellectual superiority evoked his unqualified admiration—one who loved him with her whole heart and soul, and was the heroine of at least two of the most vivid and tenderly passionate lyrics that came from his pen."

—ROBERT FORD.

Dedicated to

THE OFFICERS AND MEMBERS OF

THE EDINBURGH BURNS CLUB

BY

A SCOT ABROAD WHO IS PROUD OF HIS BEING A

NATIVE OF THEIR ILLUSTRIOUS CITY.

JOHN D. ROSS.

PREFACE.

ONE of the most pleasing results of the spread of the Burns cult is the painstaking manner in which the lives and characters of most of those who had any influence in shaping his career have been investigated and made clear to us. Even the lives of those who have been merely casually mentioned in his writings have been made the object of careful study, until now the student of the poet's earthly journey, and of the magnificent legacy he bequeathed to Scotland and the world, not only understands what manner of man he was, but is able to estimate the value to him of his mission to the men—and the women—with whom he associated in all the varied phases of his brief but memorable career.

As a result of all this scrutiny and investigation, which may be said to have started as the echoes of the birthday centennial of 1859 began to die away, we know much better than Burns students did before that year the character of the people to whom our country's poet gave his friendship, his respect, his admiration, and his love. Some have suffered in the fierce light which editors and commentators, anxious to present to the world something new, have brought to bear upon lives which, but for his eminence, would long since have passed into such utter forgetfulness as not to leave even a memory behind. We do not, for instance, think so pleasantly now of William Nicol as we did when we simply knew him as the brewer of that "peck o' maut" which still enlivens many a brewing all over the world; and we have a higher regard, now that we have learned more about him, for the memory of John Wilson, Session Clerk of Tarbolton and afterward schoolmaster in Glasgow, than we did when we knew him only as the subject of that merciless satire, "Death and Dr Hornbook."

So too with the women who were his charmers, his friends, his advisers. Year by year the fitness of Bonnie Jean to be his life companion has been more acknowledged, while the halo of romance with which he has invested her memory makes her, as the seasons roll, take a higher and tenderer place in our national literature as an inspirer of song, a heroine of poetry. So too, possibly in a more marked degree, has been the development of the reverence for the memory of " Highland Mary," which found its most recent public expression in the statue erected last year at Dunoon.

The present volume deals with another of the loves of Burns—the hapless Clarinda. It is safe to say that the memory of this gifted but unfortunate woman is held in high esteem for her genuine worth more than it was forty years ago. Then it was clouded, because people did not understand, did not have the means of understanding, her character, her career, or the story of her innocent intimacy with the poet. Since then her life-story has been searched, been weighed, been commented on ; the closest scrutiny has been bestowed on her actions, her words, her writings, and the most scalpel-like dissection has been made even of her thoughts as far as they have become recoverable. Out of all this she has emerged without a stain, with the early cloud rolled away, and with, as her only weakness, an acknowledged love for the poet in preference for the heartless scamp who wrecked her life. She once hoped that she might in time be united to the poet, but she never forgot that she was a wedded wife. To her faithless husband she remained loyal, to her children she was a model mother, and to the end of her long life's journey she enjoyed the respect of her wide circle of devoted friends.

This is brought out very clearly in the present volume, in which the story of her career is told by various writers, and the various incidents in that career — notably of course the "Burns incident" as it has been called—more or less critically analysed. The volume is in reality a tribute to the memory of Clarinda. It could have been made much larger, its size could have been swelled with ease to more stately proportions, but enough has been presented, I think, to demonstrate that among the heroines of Burns, Agnes M'Lehose is not the least deserving of honour as an honest, a beautiful, and a gifted woman.

JOHN D. ROSS.

NEW YORK,
25th January 1897.

CONTENTS.

MEMOIR OF MRS M'LEHOSE.

BY HER GRANDSON,

W. C. M'LEHOSE.

A

Memoir of Mrs M'Lehose.

BY

HER GRANDSON, W. C. M'LEHOSE.

MRS M'LEHOSE, whose maiden name was
Agnes Craig, was born in Glasgow in April 1759.
She was the daughter of Mr Andrew Craig,
surgeon in that city—a gentleman of a good
family. His brother was the Rev. William
Craig, one of the ministers of Glasgow, and
father of Lord Craig, a judge of the Court of
Session. The mother of Mrs M'Lehose was a
daughter of the Rev. John M'Laurin, minister of
Luss, and afterwards of St David's, Glasgow.
He was a brother of Colin M'Laurin, the cele-
brated mathematician and friend of Sir Isaac
Newton. Of the early years of Agnes Craig
but little is recorded. She was so delicate in
infancy that it was hardly expected she would
survive childhood. Yet of the four daughters
and a son she alone reached old age : all died
in childhood except her sister Margaret, who, at

the age of nineteen, became the wife of Captain
Kennedy of Kailzie, and died about a year
afterwards.   The education of Agnes Craig was
very incomplete, as all female education was
at that period, compared with the numerous
advantages possessed by young people of both
sexes in the present day.   All the education
bestowed upon her was some very imperfect in-
struction in English grammar, and that laborious
idleness called sampler-work ; even spelling was
much neglected.   The disadvantages attending
such an education she afterwards fully perceived,
and partially remedied at a period of life when
many women neglect the attainments previously
acquired, and but few persevere in the cultivation
of further knowledge.

Agnes lost her mother when she was only
eight years old ; and her only surviving sister,
Mrs Kennedy, dying about five years afterwards,
she was deprived of that compensation for a
mother's invaluable influence and superintend-
ence which might have been derived from an
elder sister's counsels.   Her mother's instruc-
tions, however, were not lost upon her ; for
many years afterwards she referred with heart-
felt gratitude to the benefit she derived from

the religious principles instilled into her by her "sainted mother."

Henceforward, till her marriage, she lived with the father—except that, for half a year, when fifteen years old, she was sent to an Edinburgh boarding-school — a practice apparently prevalent in those days as well as now—to finish that education which could not be said to have been properly begun, and had no solid foundation. This circumstance originated an acquaintance which ended in her marriage. Even at this early age she was considered one of the beauties of Glasgow, and was styled "the pretty Miss Nancy." Mr James M'Lehose, a young man of respectable connections, and a law agent in that city, had been disappointed in getting introduced to her ; and when he learned that she was going to Edinburgh, he engaged all the seats in the stage-coach, excepting the one taken for her. At that period the coach took the whole day to perform the journey between the two cities, stopping a considerable time for dinner on the road, which thus afforded Mr M'Lehose an excellent opportunity of making himself agreeable—an opportunity which he took the utmost pains to improve, and with success, being possessed of an agreeable and attractive person, and most insinuating manners. His deficiency of sound principle was hidden from general observation by great plausibility. After the return of "the pretty Miss Nancy" to Glasgow, Mr M'Lehose followed up the acquaintance thus commenced by paying her the most assiduous attention, and thus succeeded in winning her affections. Being young and inexperienced, deprived of the counsels of a mother and sister, and attached to one whom she thought possessed of every virtue, and who had shown so decided a partiality to her in a manner peculiarly calculated to please a romantic mind, she favourably received his addresses.

In this she was not encouraged by her friends, who thought that her beauty, talents, and connections entitled her to a superior match. However, she became Mrs M'Lehose in July 1776, being then only seventeen years of age, and her husband five years her senior. Their union, she always stated, was the result of disinterested affection on both sides. But this connection proved the bane of her happiness and the source of all her misfortunes. Married at so early an age, before the vivacity of youth was passed, and indeed before it was fully developed, possessed of considerable personal attractions, a ready flow of wit, a keen relish for society, in which her conversational powers fitted her to excel, and a strong love of admiration, she appears to have displeased her husband because she could not at once forego those enjoyments so natural to her time of life and situation. And he, without any cause, seems to have conceived the most unworthy jealousy, which led him to treat her with a severity most injudicious, and to one of her disposition, productive of the worst consequences.

She soon discovered the mistaken estimate she formed of her husband's character; and being of a high sanguine spirit, could ill brook the unmerited bad treatment she had received. To use her own words, in a statement which she afterwards made for the advice of her friends—"Only a short time had elapsed ere I perceived, with inexpressible regret, that our dispositions, tempers, and sentiments were so totally different as to banish all hopes of happiness. Our disagreements rose to such a height, and my husband's treatment was so harsh, that it was thought advisable by my friends a separation should take place, which accordingly followed in December 1780."

Mrs M'Lehose had at this period only two children living, having lost her first-born. A fourth was born a few months after this separation. Soon after this event her husband took her infant children away from her, in the hopes of thereby working on her maternal feelings, and forcing a reunion, which she firmly refused, being convinced that they could not live happily together. She parted with her children with extreme reluctance, her father being both able and willing to maintain her and them; while her husband had neglected his business, and entered into every species of dissipation, so that he became unable to maintain his children, and they were distributed among his relations—the youngest infant being, as soon as possible, removed from the tender care of his mother, and committed to the charge of a hireling nurse. He even prohibited her from seeing the children, to whom he knew she was devotedly attached. It required the utmost fortitude on her part to bear this cruel deprivation, but by enduring it she rendered her husband's cruel attempts

abortive. All the children died young, except
the late A. C. M'Lehose, W.S.

Immediately after the separation, she had re-
turned to her father's house with her children,
where she remained till his death, in the year
1782, two years afterwards. He judiciously left
his property to be invested in an annuity for
her behoof, entirely independent of her hus-
band, and beyond his control; and feeling it
unpleasant to remain in the same city with her
husband and his relations, and yet in a state
of alienation, Mrs M'Lehose, by the advice of
her friends, removed to Edinburgh in the same
year, 1782.

Her husband followed her soon after, on his
way to London, having formed an intention of
going abroad. He solicited an interview in
these terms: "Early to-morrow morning I leave
this country for ever, and therefore wish much
to pass one quarter of an hour with you. Upon
my word of honour, my dearest Nancy, it is
the last night you probably will ever have an
opportunity of seeing me in this world." This
appeal she refused for the following reasons:
"I consulted my friends: they advised me
against seeing him; and as I thought it could

be productive of no good, I declined the interview." The treatment she received from her husband while living with him must have been bad indeed to make one of her forgiving disposition so unyielding, and he seems to have been not altogether insensible to his misconduct, for two years later, and just previous to going abroad, he wrote to his wife: "For my own part, I am willing to forget what is past; neither do I require any apology from you; for I am heartily sorry for those instances of my behaviour to you which caused our separation. Were it possible to recall them, they should never be repeated." These feelings may have been sincere at the moment, but they had no depth or endurance.

Soon after Mr M'Lehose went to London, in the year 1782 he wrote his wife a very reproachful letter, stating his intention of going abroad, and bidding her take her children home to her. In this letter he observed: "The sooner you return to Glasgow the better, and take under your care and protection those endearing pledges of our once-happier days, as none of my friends will have anything to do with them." After speaking of his prospects of employment, he added: "Yet still, however remote my residence may be from you and those endearing infants, God forbid that I should be so destitute of natural affection for them, as to permit you or them, in the smallest degree, to be burdensome to any of your friends. On the contrary, I shall at all times observe the strictest economy, and exert myself to the uttermost, so that I may be enabled to contribute to your ease and happiness."

It will be seen in the sequel how this fair promise was observed. The truth is that as he could not prevail on his wife to live with him, even by depriving her of her children, to whom she was tenderly attached, and his relations would no longer support him in his idleness, or his children for his sake, their sympathy for him being blunted, if not deadened, by his misconduct, he thus contrived to throw the burden of them on his young wife, whose patrimonial income was very limited. Her situation at this trying period is thus related : " The income left me by my father being barely sufficient to board myself, I was now distressed how to support my three infants. With my spirits sunk in deep dejection, I went to Glasgow to see them. I found arrears due for their board. This I

paid ; and the goodness of some worthy gentle-
men in Glasgow procuring me a small annuity
from the writers, and one from the surgeons,
I again set out for Edinburgh with them in
August 1782 ; and by the strictest economy,
made my little income go as far as possible.
The deficiency was always supplied by some
worthy benevolent friends, whose kindness no
time can erase from my grateful heart."

When Mrs M'Lehose settled in Edinburgh
in 1782, though comparatively a stranger, her
youth, beauty, and misfortunes, and above all,
her exemplary conduct, procured for her the
friendship, not only of her own relations, but of
many respectable families, till then unknown to
her, from whom she received many substantial
proofs of kindness. Thus, though deprived of
his assistance to whom she had the most sacred
claim, she had much reason to bless God for
His goodness in raising up so many friends.
Among these friends, Lord Craig, her cousin-
german, then an advocate at the Scottish bar,
is particularly deserving of mention. He be-
friended her from her first arrival in Edinburgh,
and continued, during his life, her greatest
benefactor. Mrs M'Lehose consulted him on

all occasions of difficulty; and when deprived
of the annuities from Glasgow, soon after her
husband settled in Jamaica, on account of his
ability to maintain his children himself, Lord
Craig generously continued them, and made up
the deficiencies of her income. At his death
he left her an annuity, and made her son
residuary legatee. Besides these substantial
acts of kindness, she enjoyed his friendship,
and was a frequent visitor at his house, where
the best literary society of Edinburgh used to
assemble. During Mrs M'Lehose's early resi-
dence in Edinburgh, when she had not joined
that social circle of which she soon became an
ornament, she devoted much time and attention
to remedying the defects of her early educa-
tion. She improved her taste by the study of
the best English authors, and became profi-
cient in English composition. Possessed of a
most retentive memory, she often quoted aptly
from those authors, both in conversation and in
her correspondence, which afterwards became
extensive, and in which she excelled. It is to
be regretted that so little of that correspond-
ence has been preserved; but Mrs M'Lehose
having survived nearly all the friends of her

early life, applications made in quarters where it was supposed her letters might have been preserved, have been unsuccessful.

It was at this period also that Mrs M'Lehose began cultivating the Muses. She produced many short poetical effusions, a few of which have been preserved. Her earliest composition was an "Address to a Blackbird," which she heard singing on a tree near her residence, in the neighbourhood of a spot where St Margaret's Convent has since been placed. The ideas, she stated, came into her mind like inspiration.

In the rearing and education of her children she took great delight; and the society of the many friends she acquired yielded her constant enjoyment for a long series of years, until the progress of time thinned their ranks, and increasing years and infirmities made her, in some degree, willing to relinquish social intercourse, of which she was so fond, for the retirement befitting old age. Among the literary men who used to visit her, Thomas Campbell, who was then prosecuting his studies at the University; the amiable Graham, the author of "The Sabbath"; James Gray, author of "Cuna of Cheyd," and "The Sabbath among the Mountains "; and Robert Ainslie, the friend of Burns, author of various religious works addressed to the young, and of a series of political letters, may be enumerated. This gentleman proved throughout life a warm and steady friend. He was an original visitor at Mrs M'Lehose's New Year parties, which were kept up for about forty years, and are still remembered by several of the younger guests for their great conviviality, to which the liveliness and vivacity of the hostess greatly contributed.

Toward the end of the year 1787, Robert Burns was introduced to Mrs M'Lehose in the house of a mutual friend, Miss Nimmo. They spent the evening together ; and we have the sentiments recorded by both parties of the impressions reciprocally produced. The poet declared, in one of his letters to her : " Of all God's creatures I ever could approach in the beaten way of friendship, you struck me with the deepest, the strongest, the most permanent impression." While she wrote : " Miss Nimmo can tell you how earnestly I had long pressed her to make us acquainted. I had a presentiment that we would derive pleasure from the society of each other." The poet was at this time preparing to depart from Edinburgh; and under these circumstances, could only regret that he had not possessed the opportunity of cultivating the lady's acquaintance earlier; but a severe accident, which happened a day or two later, when he was engaged to spend the evening with her, delayed his departure for some time, and led to a correspondence in which Mrs M'Lehose fancifully adopted the name of " Clarinda," and Burns followed up the idea by signing " Sylvander." As soon as he recovered from his accident, the poet visited the lady, and they enjoyed much of each other's society for several months till he left Edinburgh. They met only once afterwards, in the year 1791, but occasionally corresponded till within a short period of his death.

When Mr M'Lehose went to London in 1782, he found too many opportunities for indulging in dissipation and extravagance to go abroad so long as he was able to procure money from his family in Scotland—assistance which they could ill afford, and were obliged finally to refuse, their patience and generosity being exhausted. After two years and a half thus spent in idleness, Mr M'Lehose was thrown into prison for debt; and his relatives, being once more appealed to, consented to advance the funds necessary for his release and outfit, on condition that he immediately went abroad. With this he complied, and sailed for Jamaica in November 1784. Before leaving London, and afterwards from Jamaica, where he became very prosperous, he wrote his mother and family most grateful letters for their kindness, but never repaid the debt, though appealed to, when his mother's income became inadequate to her support.

Mr M'Lehose did not favour his wife even with grateful letters, though she wrote him repeatedly respecting her circumstances and the health of their children. The following appeal to him from Lord Craig was equally fruitless: "I write you this letter to represent to you the situation of your family here. Your wife's father left some property in Glasgow, the interest of which your wife draws for the support of herself and children; but this not being sufficient, by the solicitation of some of your friends £8 a year was obtained from the surgeons, and £10 a year from the writers in Glasgow. Even this, however, did not do, owing to the great rise in the expense of housekeeping, and the necessary outlay for your children and their education; so that I advanced money to Mrs M. even while she got the above sums. Accounts, I am informed, have lately arrived from Jamaica which I am very glad of, representing you to be in a very good situation, and as having got into very profitable business. The surgeons and writers have withdrawn their allowance, and I have been told their principal reason for doing so is the accounts they have heard of the goodness of your situation. No remittances, however, have as yet come from you; and in this last year, owing to the withdrawal of the writers and surgeons, I have paid Mrs M'Lehose upwards of £30 above what I have received. No person, except my brother, is willing to contribute anything; and all your own relations have positively refused, from the beginning, to contribute a single farthing. In this situation I am resolved to advance no more money out of my own funds on the account of your family. What I have already given, I have never laid my account in being reimbursed, and it shall never be thought of; but for the future every consideration demands that you should yourself contribute for the support of your own children. I expect, therefore, that you will by the first opportunity write to some of your correspondents in this country, giving what directions you think proper about your children, and making some proper remittance on their account, as, I repeat it again, I am determined not to continue to pay money on their account."

In Mrs M'Lehose's narrative she states: " About the year 1787, my youngest boy, William, fell into ill-health. This increased my expense; and at this period the annuities from Glasgow were withheld from me, the reason assigned being that Mr M'Lehose was doing well, and in a way to support his children himself. I wrote once more to him, giving him an account of his children, particularly of William's helpless situation, and also my reduced circumstances, warmly expostulating with him on the duty and necessity of remitting for their support and education. I anxiously waited for an answer, but received none. In August 1788 my delicate child was happily delivered from his sufferings. I wrote again immediately of his death. Still I received no answer till the following August, when I had a letter, and soon after another, inviting me to come to Jamaica, and enclosing a bill for £50, which was meant, I suppose, to equip me, and containing the most flattering directions to give his only surviving son the best education Edinburgh would afford." "With regard to my dear son," Mr M'Lehose writes, "it is my wish that he should be placed in the first boarding-school for young gentlemen, either in Edinburgh or its environs. Whatever expense may attend it shall be regularly and punctually paid. It is my wish that he should continue at the Latin until he is perfect master of that language; and when that is accomplished, I wish him to be instructed in the French, which is now become so generally useful all over the globe, and in particular here, where I intend to fix him in business. It will be proper also that he be immediately put under a dancing-master, and, what is still more requisite, that he should learn to fence. No expense can be incurred that will not be discharged with infinite pleasure and satisfaction, provided he is to benefit by it as I could wish.

If you have no inclination to come out to this country, I then have to request you to embrace the first opportunity to inform me of such determination, as in that case I will immediately order my son up to London, and put him under the care of one of the first West India houses in the city to receive the remainder of his education either at Westminster or at Eton, whichever they think most advisable."

Mrs M'Lehose was much at a loss how to act. At first she felt strongly inclined to remain in this country, but finally resolved to proceed to Jamaica. " I consulted my friends ; they declined giving any advice, and referred me to my own mind. After much agitation, and deep and anxious reflection for my only child's sake, for whom he promised such liberal things, and encouraged by flattering accounts of his character and conduct in Jamaica, I resolved to undertake the arduous voyage."

The motives which influenced her will best be seen from the letter which she wrote to her friend, Lord Craig, upon the subject: " When I last wrote you, the bidding adieu to my dear boy was my only source of anxiety. I had then no idea whatever of going out to Mr M'Lehose.

Next day I learned from Mrs Adair that Captain Liddel told her my husband had the strongest resolution of using me kindly, in case I accepted of his invitation ; and that pride alone hindered his acknowledging his faults a second time, still hurt at my not answering his overtures of reconciliation from London. But that, in case I did not choose to come over, I might rest assured I never would hear from him while he existed. Captain Liddel added his opinion, that I ought to go, in the strongest terms. Mrs Adair joins him ; and above all, my poor son adds his entreaties most earnestly. I thought it prudent to inform him, for the first time, of the disagreement between his parents, and the unhappy jealousy in his father's temper. Still he argues that his father may be incensed at my refusal. If I go, I have a terror of the sea, and no less of the climate ; above all, the horror of again involving myself in misery in the midst of strangers, and almost without remedy. If I refuse, I must bid my only child (in whom all affections and hopes are entirely centred) adieu for ever : struggle with a straitened income and the world's censure solitary and unprotected. The bright side of these alternatives is, that if

I go my husband's jealousy of temper may be abated, from a better knowledge of the world; and time and misfortunes, by making alterations both on person and vivacity, will render me less likely to incur his suspicions; and that ill humour, which partly arose from straitened fortune, will be removed by affluence. I will enjoy my son's society, and have him for a friend; and who knows what effect so fine a boy may have on a father long absent from his sight. If I refuse, and stay here, I shall continue to enjoy a circle of kind, respectable friends. Though my income be small, I can never be in want, and I shall maintain that liberty which, after nine years' enjoyment, I shall find it hard to forego, even to the degree to which I am sensible every married woman must submit."

A few days later she wrote again to the same gentleman: "On Friday last I went down to Leith, and had a conversation on board the 'Roselle' with Captain Liddel. He told me that Mr M'Lehose had talked of me, and of my coming over, with great tenderness; and said it would be my fault if we did not enjoy great happiness; and concluded with assuring me, if I were his own child he would advise me to go out. This conversation has tended greatly to decide my accepting my husband's invitation. I have done what you desired me—weighed coolly (as coolly as a subject so interesting would permit) all I have to suffer or expect in either situation ; and the result is, my going to Jamaica. This appears to me the preferable choice ; it is surely the path of duty ; and such, I may look for the blessing of God to attend my endeavours for happiness with him who was the husband of my choice and the father of my children. On Saturday I was agreeably surprised by a call from Mr Kemp. He had received my letter that morning at Glasgow, and had alighted for a few minutes, on his way to Easter Dudding-ston, where his family are for summer quarters. He was much affected with my perplexing situation. Like you, he knew not how to decide, and left me, promising to call early this day, which he has done. I told him of the meeting with Mr Liddel, and enumerated all the arguments which I had thought of on both sides of the question. What Mr Liddel (who is a man of known worth) said to me weighed much with him ; and he, too, is now of opinion my going to Jamaica is advisable. He gave me much good advice as to my conduct towards Mr M'Lehose, and promised to write him himself. Your letter luckily arrived while he was with me. The assurance of my little income being secured me not a little adds both to his opinion of the propriety of my going, and to my ease and comfort, in case (after doing all I can) it should prove impossible to enjoy that peace which I so earnestly pant after ; and I would fain hope for a tender reception. After ten years' separation, and the sacrifice I make bidding adieu (probably for ever) to my friends and my country—indeed, I am much depressed in mind—should I escape the sea, the climate may prove fatal to me ; but should it happen so, I have the satisfaction to think I shall die in attempting to attain happiness in that path of duty which Providence and a succession of events seem to point out for the best. You, my dear kind benefactor, have had much trouble with me first and last ; and though others appear ungrateful, neither time nor absence can ever erase from my heart the remembrance of your past kindness. My prayers shall ascend for the reward of Heaven upon your head. To-morrow I am to write to my husband. Mr Kemp is to see it on Wednesday. If any person occurs to you as proper to place Andrew with in Edinburgh, let me know—the sooner the better : the hopes of his rejoining me will help to console my mind in the midst of strangers. I am sorry you are to be so long of coming to town. Meantime I shall be glad to hear from you : for I am, my dear Sir, in every possible situation, your affectionate and obliged friend, A. M."

" I accordingly wrote my husband in October 1791, acquainting him with my resolution of forgetting past differences, and throwing myself on his protection." As the " Roselle" did not leave for Jamaica till spring, she again wrote him in December.

After giving the details of the arrangements she had made for their son's education, in compliance with his instructions, she thus proceeds : " I had occasion to be in Glasgow lately for two days only. I called for your mother. I felt much for her—bereaved of so many children. The peculiar circumstances which attended poor Annie's death affected me excessively. They told me you had not written these three years past ; but I assured them (and I hope it is the case) that your letters must have miscarried, as

I could not believe you capable of such unkind neglect. I am certain, inclination, no less than duty, must ever prompt you to pay attention to your mother. She has met with many and sore afflictions, and I feel for her the most sincere sympathy." In the same letter she adds: " I have met with much kindness since I came to Edinburgh, from a set of most agreeable and respectable friends. No ideas of wealth or splendour could compensate for the pain I shall feel in bidding them adieu. Nothing could support me but the fond reliance I have of gaining your affections and confidence. To possess these is the dearest wish of my heart, and I trust the Almighty will grant this my ardent desire. I would fain hope to hear from you ere I sail; a kind letter from you would prove a balm to my soul during the anxieties of a tedious voyage."

Mrs M'Lehose sailed from Leith in February 1792, and arrived at Kingston in April following. The day before her departure she received a letter from her fickle husband, dissuading her from going out, on the pretence that the yellow fever prevailed in the island, and that a revolt had taken place among the negroes; both of which statements were false. But having taken leave of her friends, engaged her passage, and made the preparations which the expectation of an absence, prolonged perhaps for years, required, she resolved (unwisely, as the event proved) to proceed. It is a curious coincidence that the vessel she sailed in was the " Roselle," the same in which Burns intended to have sailed for the same destination a few years earlier.

Mrs M'Lehose suffered much from the voyage, especially in the warmer latitudes, and when she reached Kingston, her husband did not go down to the ship for a length of time. All the other lady passengers had been speedily joined by their friends. When he came, he was very cold, and seemed far from being glad to see his wife ; and even in this interview, before they left the ship, he used some harsh expressions towards her in presence of the captain and others which wounded her feelings much.

" As my constitution never agreed with heat, I felt its bad effects as soon as we had crossed the Line ; but the very cold reception I received from Mr M'Lehose on landing, gave me a shock which, joined to the climate, deranged my mind to such a degree as made me not answerable for what I either said or did. My husband's after-kindness could not remove the complication of nervous disorders which seized me. They increased to such a height that Dr Fife, the professional gentleman who attended me, and whose soothing manner I can never forget, was of opinion my going home was absolutely necessary—otherwise my reason, if not my life, would fall a sacrifice. Accordingly, in June I took leave of Mr M'Lehose, and returned home in the ship I had gone out in. Our parting was most affectionate. On my part, it was with sincere regret that my health obliged me to leave him. Upon his, it was to all appearance equally so. However, we parted with mutual promises of constancy, and of keeping up a regular correspondence. After getting into cool air, I gradually recovered my health."

There were other reasons for leaving Jamaica besides those which she mentioned in the statement just quoted. Mr M'Lehose, like most West Indian planters, had a family by a coloured mistress. This could not be otherwise than a source of mortification and annoyance. The ebullition of temper which he had exhibited towards her on their first meeting was a prelude to more violent outbreaks, which, though not always directed to her personally, paralysed her with fear. His slaves were generally the objects of these fits of wrath; and seeing that his wife pitied their abject condition, he took pleasure in threatening and abusing them in her presence.

Circumstances were thus most unfavourable to Mrs M'Lehose's stay in Jamaica; but, had they been propitious, she was ill calculated to endure a permanent change of habits. That she was undoubtedly very unhappy in the West Indies may be gathered from the following extract from her journal many years afterwards: " Recollect that I arrived in Jamaica this day twenty-two years. What I suffered during the three months I remained there, Lord, make me grateful for Thy goodness in bringing me back to my native country."

Mrs M'Lehose arrived in Edinburgh in August 1792, and soon after resumed housekeeping, and took home her son, who had been placed at Dr Chapman's excellent boarding-school. The first year had now expired without any part of the expense being defrayed by his father, and the debt was ultimately cancelled by the liberality of Lord Craig. As Mr M'Lehose continued thus utterly to neglect his wife and son, she was prevailed on by her friends to institute proceedings against him before the Court of Session in order to enforce these obligations. In March 1797, accordingly, she obtained a judgment of the Court, ordaining him to pay her a yearly aliment of £100 sterling. From that judgment the following is an extract: "In the close of the year 1784, Mr M'Lehose settled as an attorney-at-law in Kingston, Jamaica; and business increased so rapidly, that he was soon in possession of, and still enjoys, a revenue of £1,000 a year from his profession."

This decree, however, owing to Mr M'Lehose being resident in Jamaica, did not add to Mrs M'Lehose's income; although it was the means ultimately of enabling her to recover in this country some funds belonging to her husband. Thus abandoned by her husband, Mrs M'Lehose and her only son, the late Mr Andrew M'Lehose, W.S., continued to live together. Soon after her return from Jamaica, Mr Robert Ainslie, the friend of Burns, kindly took her son as apprentice. He continued to live with his mother until the year 1809, when he married. They lived most happily together; and probably there have been few instances of more devoted mutual attachment between parent and child.

In March 1812, Mr M'Lehose died at Kingston ; and though he had been in receipt of a large income for many years as Chief Clerk of the Court of Common Pleas in Jamaica, no funds were ever received from that island by his family. A report reached this country, as being a matter of notoriety in Kingston, that some of his particular friends had, on the approach of death, sent all his domestics out of the house, and as soon as the breath quitted his body, carried off whatever cash and documents there were. If so, the friends proved befitting the man. Notice, however, was given to Mrs M'Lehose that a balance of several hundred pounds, belonging to her husband, was in the hands of Messrs Coutts in London, which she soon afterwards obtained.

It was then discovered that he had had an account current at this bank for many years, while he had suffered his family to have their income eked out by the generosity of friends : £50 advanced to her, as already mentioned, before she sailed for Jamaica, and a present of £21 on leaving that island, being all which this wealthy husband bestowed on his family in the long period of thirty-two years. Yet, after her departure from Jamaica, he was in the habit of speaking of his family with great affection, and boasted of the valuable presents which he had made his wife and son. It is known that he was a man of talents and pleasing address, but his temper was occasionally violent and ungovernable. Yet he was often soft and agreeable. His written correspondence showed the same characteristics—alternate passages of the most endearing and the most insulting language.

LETTERS TO MRS M‘LEHOSE.

Letters to Mrs M'Lehose.

No. I.

To Mrs M'Lehose.

Tuesday Evening [*December* 6, 1787].

Madam,

I had set no small store by my tea-drinking to-night, and have not often been so disappointed. Saturday evening I shall embrace the opportunity with the greatest pleasure. I leave town this day se'nnight, and probably for a couple of twelvemonths ; but must ever regret that I so lately got an acquaintance I shall ever highly esteem, and in whose welfare I shall ever be warmly interested.

Our worthy common friend, in her usual pleasant way, rallied me a good deal on my new acquaintance, and in the humour of her ideas I wrote some lines, which I enclose you,

as I think they have a good deal of poetic
merit; and Miss [Nimmo] tells me you are
not only a critic, but a poetess. Fiction, you
know, is the native region of poetry; and I
hope you will pardon my vanity in sending
you the bagatelle as a tolerable off-hand *jeu
d'esprit.* I have several poetic trifles, which I
will gladly leave with Miss [Nimmo] or you, if
they were worth house-room; as there are
scarcely two people on earth by whom it would
mortify me more to be forgotten, though at
the distance of ninescore miles.

I am, Madam, with the highest respect,

Your very humble Servant,

* * * *

No. II.

To Mrs M'Lehose.

Saturday Even [*December* 8].

I can say with truth, Madam, that I never
met with a person in my life whom I more
anxiously wished to meet again than yourself.
To-night I was to have had that very great

pleasure—I was intoxicated with the idea ; but an unlucky fall from a coach has so bruised one of my knees, that I can't stir my leg off the cushion. So, if I don't see you again, I shall not rest in my grave for chagrin. I was vexed to the soul I had not seen you sooner. I determined to cultivate your friendship with the enthusiasm of religion ; but thus has Fortune ever served me. I cannot bear the idea of leaving Edinburgh without seeing you. I know not how to account for it—I am strangely taken with some people, nor am I often mistaken. You are a stranger to me ; but I am an odd being. Some yet unnamed feelings—things, not principles, but better than whims—carry me farther than boasted reason ever did a philosopher.

Farewell ! every happiness be yours.

ROBERT BURNS.

No. III.

To Mrs M'Lehose.

I STRETCH a point indeed, my dearest Madam, when I answer your card on the rack of my

present agony. Your friendship, Madam! By
heavens, I was never proud before! Your lines,
I maintain it, are poetry, and good poetry;
mine were indeed partly fiction, and partly a
friendship which, had I been so blest as to
have met with you *in time*, might have led me
—God of love only knows where. Time is too
short for ceremonies.

I swear solemnly (in all the tenor of my
former oath) to remember you in all the pride
and warmth of friendship until—I cease to be!

To-morrow, and every day, till I see you, you
shall hear from me.

Farewell! May you enjoy a better night's
repose than I am likely to have!

No. IV.

To Mrs M'Lehose.

YOUR last, my dear Madam, had the effect on
me that Job's situation had on his friends, when
"they sat down seven days and seven nights
astonied, and spake not a word." "Pay my
addresses to a married woman!" I started as
if I had seen the ghost of him I had injured:

I recollected my expressions; some of them indeed were, in the law phrase, "habit and repute," which is being half guilty. I cannot positively say, Madam, whether my heart might not have gone astray a little; but I can declare, upon the honour of a poet, that the vagrant has wandered unknown to me. I have a pretty handsome troop of follies of my own; and, like some other people's retinue, they are but un-disciplined blackguards; but the luckless rascals have something of honour in them: they would not do a dishonest thing.

To meet with an unfortunate woman, amiable and young, deserted and widowed by those who were bound by every tie of duty, nature, and gratitude to protect, comfort, and cherish her; add to all, when she is perhaps one of the first of lovely forms and noble minds, the mind, too, that hits one's taste as the joys of heaven do a saint—should a vague infant idea, the natural child of imagination, thoughtlessly peep over the fence—were you, my friend, to sit in judgment, and the poor, airy straggler brought before you, trembling, self-condemned, with artless eyes, brimful of contrition, looking wistfully on its judge, you could not, my dear

Madam, condemn the hapless wretch to death "without benefit of clergy"?

I won't tell you what reply my heart made to your raillery of "seven years": but I will give you what a brother of my trade says on the same allusion :—

> "The Patriarch to gain a wife,
>   Chaste, beautiful and young,
> Served fourteen years a painful life,
>   And never thought it long.
>
> "Oh, were you to reward such cares,
>   And life so long would stay,
> Not fourteen but four hundred years
>   Would seem as but one day."

I have written you this scrawl because I have nothing else to do, and you may sit down and find fault with it, if you have no better way of consuming your time; but finding fault with the vagaries of a poet's fancy is much such another business as Xerxes chastising the waves of the Hellespont.

My limb now allows me to sit in some peace: to walk I have yet no prospect of, as I can't mark it to the ground.

I have just now looked over what I have written, and it is such a chaos of nonsense that

I daresay you will throw it into the fire, and call me an idle, stupid fellow; but whatever you may think of my brains, believe me to be, with the most sacred respect and heartfelt esteem,

My dear Madam, your humble Servant,

ROBERT BURNS.

No. V.

TO CLARINDA.

Friday Evening [*December* 21].

I BEG your pardon, my dear " Clarinda," for the fragment scrawl I sent you yesterday. I really do not know what I wrote. A gentleman for whose character, abilities, and critical know-ledge I have the highest veneration, called in just as I had begun the second sentence, and I would not make the porter wait. I read to my much-respected friend several of my own baga-telles, and, among others, your lines, which I had copied out. He began some criticisms on them as on the other pieces, when I informed him they were the work of a young lady in this town, which, I assure you, made him stare. My learned friend seriously protested that he did

not believe any young woman in Edinburgh
was capable of such lines; and if you know
anything of Professor Gregory, you will neither
doubt of his abilities nor his sincerity. I do
love you, if possible, still better for having so
fine a taste and turn for poesy. I have again
gone wrong in my usual unguarded way, but
you may erase the word, and put esteem, respect,
or any other tame Dutch expression you please
in its place. I believe there is no holding con-
verse, or carrying on correspondence, with an
amiable woman, much less a *gloriously amiable
fine woman*, without some mixture of that
delicious passion whose most devoted slave I
have more than once had the honour of being.
But why be hurt or offended on that account?
Can no honest man have a prepossession for a
fine woman, but he must run his head against
an intrigue? Take a little of the tender witch-
craft of love, and add to it the generous, the
honourable sentiments of manly friendship, and
I know but *one* more delightful morsel, which
few, few in any rank ever taste. Such a com-
position is like adding cream to strawberries:
it not only gives the fruit a more elegant rich-
ness, but has a peculiar deliciousness of its own.

I enclose you a few lines I composed on a late melancholy occasion.* I will not give above five or six copies of it at all, and I would be hurt if any friend should give any copies without my consent.

You cannot imagine, Clarinda (I like the idea of Arcadian names in a commerce of this kind), how much store I have set by the hopes of your future friendship. I do not know if you have a just idea of my character, but I wish you to see me as I am. I am, as most people of my trade are, a strange Will-o'-wisp being; the victim, too frequently, of much imprudence and many follies. My great constituent elements are *pride* and *passion*. The first I have endeavoured to humanise into integrity and honour; the last makes me a devotee to the warmest degree of enthusiasm in love, religion, or friendship— either of them, or all together, as I happen to be inspired. 'Tis true I never saw you but once; but how much acquaintance did I form with you in that once! Do not think I flatter you, or have a design upon you, Clarinda: I have too

---

* Probably the verses on the Death of the Lord President.

much pride for the one, and too little cold
contrivance for the other; but of all God's
creatures I ever could approach in the beaten
way of my acquaintance, you struck me with the
deepest, the strongest, the most permanent im-
pression. I say the most permanent, because I
know myself well, and how far I can promise
either in my prepossessions or powers. Why
are you unhappy? And why are so many of
our fellow-creatures, unworthy to belong to the
same species with you, blest with all they can
wish? You have a hand all benevolent to give:
why were you denied the pleasure? You have
a heart formed—gloriously formed—for all the
most refined luxuries of love: why was that
heart ever wrung? Oh Clarinda! shall we not
meet in a state, some yet unknown state of
being, where the lavish hand of plenty shall
minister to the highest wish of benevolence, and
where the chill north wind of prudence shall
never blow over the flowery fields of enjoyment?
If we do not, man was made in vain! I deserve
most of the unhappy hours that have lingered
over my head; they were the wages of my
labour: but what unprovoked demon, malignant
as hell, stole upon the confidence of unmistrust-

ing busy fate, and dashed *your* cup of life with
undeserved sorrow?

Let me know how long your stay will be out
of town; I shall count the hours till you inform
me of your return. Cursed *etiquette* forbids your
seeing me just now; and so soon as I can walk
I must bid Edinburgh adieu. Lord! why was I
born to see misery which I cannot relieve, and
to meet with friends whom I cannot enjoy? I
look back with the pang of unavailing avarice
on my loss in not knowing you sooner: all last
winter, these three months past, what luxury of
intercourse have I not lost! Perhaps, though,
'twas better for my peace. You see I am either
above or incapable of dissimulation. I believe
it is want of that particular genius. I despise
design, because I want either coolness or wisdom
to be capable of it. I am interrupted. Adieu,
my dear Clarinda!

SYLVANDER.

No. VI.

To Clarinda.

My dear Clarinda,

Your last verses have so delighted me, that
I have copied them in among some of my own

most valued pieces, which I keep sacred for my own use. Do let me have a few now and then.

Did you, Madam, know what I feel when you talk of your sorrows !

Good God ! that one who has so much worth in the sight of Heaven, and is so amiable to her fellow-creatures, should be so unhappy. I can't venture out for cold. My limb is vastly better ; but I have not any use of it without my crutches. Monday, for the first time, I dine at a neighbour's, next door. As soon as I can go so far, *even in a coach*, my first visit shall be to you. Write me when you leave town, and immediately when you return ; and I earnestly pray your stay may be short. You can't imagine how miserable you made me when you hinted to me not to write. Farewell.

SYLVANDER.

No. VII.

TO CLARINDA.

[*After New Year's Day*, 1788.]

YOU are right, my dear Clarinda : a friendly correspondence goes for nothing, except one write their undisguised sentiments. Yours please me for their intrinsic merit, as well as because they are *yours*, which, I assure you, is to me a high recommendation. Your religious sentiments, Madam, I revere. If you have, on some suspicious evidence, from some lying oracle learned that I despise or ridicule so sacredly important a matter as real religion, you have, my Clarinda, much misconstrued your friend ;— "I am not mad, most noble Festus!" Have you ever met a perfect character? Do we not sometimes rather exchange faults than get rid of them? For instance, I am perhaps tired with and shocked at a life too much the prey of giddy inconsistencies and thoughtless follies ; by degrees I grow sober, prudent, and statedly pious—I say statedly, because the most unaffected devotion is not at all inconsistent with my first character—I join the world in congratulating myself on the happy change. But let me pry more narrowly into this affair. Have I, at bottom, anything of a secret pride in these endowments and emendations? Have I nothing of a Presbyterian sourness, a hypocritical severity, when I survey my less regular neighbours? In a word, have I missed all those nameless and numberless modifications of indistinct selfishness

D

which are so near our own eyes, we can scarcely bring them within the sphere of our vision, and which the known spotless cambric of our character hides from the ordinary observer.

My definition of worth is short: truth and humanity respecting our fellow-creatures; reverence and humility in the presence of that Being, my Creator and Preserver, and who, I have every reason to believe, will one day be my Judge. The first part of my definition is the creature of unbiassed instinct; the last is the child of after reflection. Where I found these two essentials, I would gently note, and slightly mention, any attendant flaws—flaws, the marks, the consequences of human nature.

I can easily enter into the sublime pleasures that your strong imagination and keen sensibility must derive from religion, particularly if a little in the shade of misfortune; but I own I cannot, without a marked grudge, see Heaven totally engross so amiable, so charming a woman, as my friend Clarinda; and should be very well pleased at *a circumstance* that would put it in the power of somebody (happy somebody!) to divide her attention, with all the delicacy and tenderness of an earthly attachment.

You will not easily persuade me that you have not a grammatical knowledge of the English language. So far from being inaccurate, you are elegant beyond any woman of my acquaintance, except one, whom I wish you knew.

Your last verses to me have so delighted me, that I have got an excellent old Scots air that suits the measure, and you shall see them in print in the "Scots Musical Museum," a work publishing by a friend of mine in this town. I want four stanzas; you gave me but three, and one of them alluded to an expression in my former letter; so I have taken your two first verses, with a slight alteration in the second, and have added a third; but you must help me to a fourth. Here they are: the latter half of the first stanza would have been worthy of Sappho; I am in raptures with it.

> " Talk not of Love, it gives me pain,
>   For Love has been my foe :
>   He bound me with an iron chain,
>   And sunk me deep in woe.
>
> " But Friendship's pure and lasting joys
>   My heart was form'd to prove :
>   There, welcome, win and wear the prize,
>   But never talk of love."

Your friendship much can make me blest,
   O why that bliss destroy?
       [only]
Why urge the odious one request,
       [will]
   You know I must deny?

The alteration in the second stanza is no improvement, but there was a slight inaccuracy in your rhyme. The third I only offer to your choice, and have left two words for your determination. The air is "The Banks of Spey," and is most beautiful.

To-morrow evening I intend taking a chair, and paying a visit at Park Place to a much-valued old friend. If I could be sure of finding you at home (and I will send one of the chairmen to call), I would spend from five to six o'clock with you, as I go past. I cannot do more at this time, as I have something on my hand that hurries me much. I propose giving you the first call, my old friend the second, and Miss ——, as I return home. Do not break any engagement for me, as I will spend another evening with you at any rate before I leave town.

Do not tell me that you are pleased when your friends inform you of your faults. I am ignorant what they are; but I am sure they must be such evanescent trifles, compared with your personal and mental accomplishments, that I would despise the ungenerous narrow soul who would notice any shadow of imperfections you may seem to have any other way than in the most delicate agreeable raillery. Coarse minds are not aware how much they injure the keenly-feeling tie of bosom-friendship, when, in their foolish officiousness, they mention what nobody cares for recollecting. People of nice sensibility and generous minds have a certain intrinsic dignity, that fires at being trifled with, or lowered, or even too nearly approached.

You need make no apology for long letters: I am even with you. Many happy new-years to you, charming Clarinda! I can't dissemble, were it to shun perdition. He who sees you as I have done, and does not love you, deserves to be damned for his stupidity! He who loves you, and would injure you, deserves to be doubly damned for his villany! Adieu.

SYLVANDER.

P.S.—What would you think of this for a fourth stanza?

Your thought, if love must harbour there,
    Conceal it in that thought,
Nor cause me from my bosom tear
    The very friend I sought.

No. VIII.

To Clarinda.

SOME days, some nights, nay, some *hours*, like the " ten righteous persons in Sodom," save the rest of the vapid, tiresome, miserable months and years of life.   One of these hours my dear Clarinda blest me with yesternight.

" One well-spent hour,
In such a tender circumstance for friends,
Is better than an age of common time !"—THOMSON.

My favourite feature in Milton's Satan is his manly fortitude in supporting what cannot be remedied—in short, the wild broken fragments of a noble exalted mind in ruins.   I meant no more by saying he was a favourite hero of mine.

I mentioned to you my letter to Dr Moore, giving an account of my life: it is truth, every word of it, and will give you a just idea of the

man whom you have honoured with your friend-
ship. I am afraid you will hardly be able to
make sense of so torn a piece. Your verses I
shall muse on deliciously, as I gaze on your
image in my mind's eye, in my heart's core:
they will be in time enough for a week to come.
I am truly happy your headache is better. Oh,
how can pain or evil be so daringly unfeeling,
cruelly savage as to wound so noble a mind, so
lovely a form!

My little fellow is all my namesake. Write
me soon. My every, strongest good wishes
attend you, Clarinda!

SYLVANDER.

I know not what I have written, I am pes-
tered with people around me.

No. IX.

To CLARINDA.

Tuesday Night [January 8?].

I AM delighted, charming Clarinda, with your
honest enthusiasm for religion. Those of either
sex, but particularly the female, who are luke-

warm in that most important of all things, "O
my soul, come not thou into their secrets!"
I feel myself deeply interested in your good
opinion, and will lay before you the outlines of
my belief. He who is our Author and Pre-
server, and will one day be our Judge, must be
(not for His sake in the way of duty, but from
the native impulse of our hearts) the object of
our reverential awe and grateful adoration; He
is almighty and all-bounteous, we are weak and
dependent; hence prayer and every other sort
of devotion.——"He is not willing that any
should perish, but that all should come to ever-
lasting life;" consequently it must be in every
one's power to embrace His offer of "everlasting
life"; otherwise He could not, in justice, con-
demn those who did not. A mind pervaded,
actuated, and governed by purity, truth, and
charity, though it does not *merit* heaven, yet is
an absolutely necessary prerequisite, without
which heaven can neither be obtained nor en-
joyed; and, by Divine promise, such a mind
shall never fail of attaining "everlasting life":
hence the impure, the deceiving, and the un-
charitable extrude themselves from eternal bliss,
by their unfitness for enjoying it. The Supreme

Being has put the immediate administration of all this, for wise and good ends known to Himself, into the hands of Jesus Christ—a great personage, whose relation to Him we cannot comprehend, but whose relation to us is [that of] a guide and Saviour; and who, except for our own obstinacy and misconduct, will bring us all through various ways, and by various means, to bliss at last.

These are my tenets, my lovely friend; and which, I think, cannot be well disputed. My creed is pretty nearly expressed in the last clause of Jamie Deans's grace, an honest weaver in Ayrshire: "Lord, grant that we may lead a gude life! for a gude life makes a gude end; at least it helps weel."

I am flattered by the entertainment you tell me you have found in my packet. You see me as I have been, you know me as I am, and may guess at what I am likely to be. I too may say, "Talk not of love," &c., for indeed he has "plunged me deep in woe!" Not that I ever saw a woman who pleased unexceptionably, as my Clarinda elegantly says, "in the companion, the friend, and the mistress." *One* indeed I could except—*one*, before passion threw its mists

over my discernment, I knew *the* first of women!
Her name is indelibly written in my heart's core
—but I dare not look in on it—a degree of
agony would be the consequence. Oh, thou
perfidious, cruel, mischief-making demon, who
presidest over that frantic passion—thou mayst,
thou dost poison my peace, but thou shalt not
taint my honour — I would not, for a single
moment, give an asylum to the most distant
imagination, that would shadow the faintest
outline of a selfish gratification, at the expense
of her whose happiness is twisted with the
threads of my existence. —— May she be as
happy as she deserves! And if my tenderest,
faithfulest friendship can add to her bliss, I shall
at least have one solid mine of enjoyment in my
bosom. *Don't guess at these ravings!*

I watched at our front window to-day, but
was disappointed.* It has been a day of disap-
pointments. I am just risen from a two hours'
bout after supper, with silly or sordid souls, who
could relish nothing in common with me but the

---

* Mrs M'Lehose had promised to pass through his
Square about two in the afternoon, and give him a nod
if he were at the window of his room and she could
discover it.

port. —— *One* —— 'Tis now "witching time of night"; and whatever is out of joint in the fore-going scrawl, impute it to enchantments and spells; for I can't look over it, but will seal it up directly, as I don't care for to-morrow's criticisms on it.

You are by this time fast asleep, Clarinda; may good angels attend and guard you as constantly as my good wishes do!

> " Beauty, which, whether waking or asleep,
> Shot forth peculiar graces."

John Milton, I wish thy soul better rest than I expect on my pillow to-night. Oh, for a little of the cart-horse part of human nature! Good-night, my dearest Clarinda!

SYLVANDER.

No. X.

TO CLARINDA.

Thursday Noon [*January* 10?].

I AM certain I saw you, Clarinda; but you don't look to the proper story for a poet's lodging—

> " Where Speculation roosted near the sky."

I could almost have thrown myself over for very

vexation. Why didn't you look higher? It has spoilt my peace for this day. To be so near my charming Clarinda; to miss her look while it was searching for me! I am sure the soul is capable of disease, for mine has convulsed itself into an inflammatory fever. I am sorry for your little boy: do let me know to-morrow how he is.

You have converted me, Clarinda (I shall love that name while I live: there is heavenly music in it!). Booth and Amelia I know well. Your sentiments on that subject, as they are on every subject, are just and noble. " To be feelingly alive to kindness and to unkindness " is a charming female character.

What I said in my last letter, the powers of fuddling sociality only know for me. By yours, I understand my good star has been partly in my horizon when I got wild in my reveries. Had that evil planet, which has almost all my life shed its baleful rays on my devoted head, been as usual in its zenith, I had certainly blabbed something that would have pointed out to you the dear object of my tenderest friend-ship, and, in spite of me, something more. Had that fatal information escaped me, and it was merely chance or kind stars that it did not,

I had been undone. You would never have written me, except, perhaps, *once* more. Oh, I could curse circumstances! and the coarse tie of human laws which keeps fast what common sense would loose, and which bars that happiness itself cannot give—happiness which otherwise love and honour would warrant! But hold —I shall make no more "hairbreadth 'scapes."

My friendship, Clarinda, is a life-rent business. My likings are both strong and eternal. I told you I had but one male friend: I have but two female. I should have a third, but she is surrounded by the blandishments of flattery and courtship. Her I register in my heart's core by Peggy Chalmers: Miss Nimmo can tell you how divine she is. She is worthy of a place in the same bosom with my Clarinda. That is the highest compliment I can pay her. Farewell, Clarinda! Remember

SYLVANDER.

No. XI.

To CLARINDA.

Saturday Morning.

YOUR thoughts on religion, Clarinda, shall be welcome. You may perhaps distrust me when

I say 'tis also my favourite topic ; but mine is the religion of the bosom. I hate the very idea of a controversial divinity ; as I firmly believe, that every honest, upright man, of whatever sect, will be accepted of the Deity. If your verses, as you seem to hint, contain censure, except you want an occasion to break with me, don't send them. I have a little infirmity in my disposition, that where I fondly love, or highly esteem, I cannot bear reproach.

"Reverence thyself" is a sacred maxim, and I wish to cherish it. I think I told you Lord Bolingbroke's saying to Swift — "Adieu, dear Swift, with all thy faults, I love thee entirely ; make an effort to love me with all mine." A glorious sentiment, and without which there can be no friendship. I do highly, very highly esteem you indeed, Clarinda—you merit it all. Perhaps, too, I scorn dissimulation. I could fondly love you ; judge, then, what a maddening sting your reproach would be. "Oh, I have sins to *Heaven*, but none to *you !*" With what pleasure would I meet you to-day, but I cannot walk to meet the Fly. I hope to be able to see you on *foot*, about the middle of next week.

I am interrupted—perhaps you are not sorry

for it, you will tell me—but I won't anticipate blame. Oh Clarinda! did you know how dear to me is your look of kindness, your smile of approbation, you would not, either in prose or verse, risk a censorious remark.

> "Curst be the verse, how well soe'er it flow,
> That tends to make one worthy man my foe!"

SYLVANDER.

No. XII.

To Clarinda.

YOU talk of weeping, Clarinda: some involuntary drops wet your lines as I read them. Offend me, my dearest angel! You cannot offend me—you never offended me. If you had ever given me the least shadow of offence, so pardon me, my God, as I forgive Clarinda. I have read yours again; it has blotted my paper. Though I find your letter has agitated me into a violent headache, I shall take a chair and be with you about eight. A friend is to be with us at tea, on my account, which hinders me from coming sooner. Forgive, my dearest Clarinda, my unguarded expressions. For Heaven's sake, forgive me, or I shall never be able to bear my own mind.

Your unhappy
SYLVANDER.

No. XIII.

TO CLARINDA.

Monday Even, 11 *o'clock.*

WHY have I not heard from you, Clarinda ? To-day I expected it; and before supper, when a letter to me was announced, my heart danced with rapture: but behold, it was some fool, who had taken it into his head to turn poet, and made me an offering of the first-fruits of his nonsense. "It is not poetry, but prose run mad." Did I ever repeat to you an epigram I made on a Mr Elphinstone, who has given a translation of Martial, a famous Latin poet ? The poetry of Elphinstone can only equal his prose notes. I was sitting in a merchant's shop of my acquaintance, waiting somebody; he put Elphinstone into my hand, and asked my opinion of it; I begged leave to write it on a blank leaf, which I did—

TO MR ELPHINSTONE, ETC.

Oh thou, whom Poesy abhors !
Whom Prose has turnèd out of doors !
Heard'st thou yon groan ?—proceed no further !
'Twas laurelled Martial calling murther !

I am determined to see you, if at all possible, on Saturday evening. Next week I must sing—

> The night is my departing night,
>   The morn's the day I maun awa';
> There's neither friend nor foe o' mine
>   But wishes that I were awa' !

> What I hae done for lack o' wit,
>   I never, never can reca';
> I hope ye're a' my friends as yet—
>   Gude night, and joy be wi' you a' !

If I could see you sooner, I would be so much the happier ; but I would not purchase the dearest gratification on earth, if it must be at your expense in worldly censure, far less inward peace.

I shall certainly be ashamed of thus scrawling whole sheets of incoherence. The only *unity* (a sad word with poets and critics !) in my ideas is CLARINDA. There my heart "reigns and revels!"

> " What art thou, Love ? whence are those charms,
>   That thus thou bear'st an universal rule ?
> For thee the soldier quits his arms,
>   The king turns slave, the wise man fool.

E

In vain we chase thee from the field,
 And with cool thoughts resist thy yoke :
Next tide of blood, alas, we yield,
 And all those high resolves are broke !"

I like to have quotations for every occasion.
They give one's ideas so pat, and save one the
trouble of finding expression adequate to one's
feelings. I think it is one of the greatest plea-
sures attending a poetic genius, that we can give
our woes, cares, joys, loves, &c., an embodied
form in verse, which to me is ever immediate
ease. Goldsmith says finely of his Muse—

" Thou source of all my bliss and all my woe,
 Thou found'st me poor at first, and keep'st me so."

My limb has been so well to-day, that I have
gone up and down stairs often without my staff.
To-morrow I hope to walk once again on my
own legs to dinner. It is only next street.
Adieu !

SYLVANDER.

No. XIV.

To Clarinda.

Tuesday Evening [*January* 15 ?].

THAT you have faults, my Clarinda, I never
doubted ; but I knew not where they existed,

and Saturday night made me more in the dark than ever. Oh Clarinda! why will you wound my soul by hinting that last night must have lessened my opinion of you? True, I was "behind the scenes" with you; but what did I see? A bosom glowing with honour and benevolence; a mind ennobled by genius, informed and refined by education and reflection, and exalted by native religion, genuine as in the climes of heaven; a heart formed for all the glorious meltings of friendship, love, and pity. These I saw: I saw the noblest immortal soul creation ever showed me.

I looked long, my dear Clarinda, for your letter; and am vexed that you are complaining. I have not caught you so far wrong as in your idea, that the commerce you have with *one* friend hurts you if you cannot tell every tittle of it to *another*. Why have so injurious a suspicion of a good God, Clarinda, as to think that Friendship and Love, on the sacred inviolate principles of Truth, Honour, and Religion, can be anything else than an object of His divine approbation?

I have mentioned in some of my former scrawls, Saturday evening next. Do allow me

to wait on you that evening.   Oh, my angel!
how soon must we part! and when can we
meet again!   I look forward on the horrid
interval with tearful eyes.   What have I lost
by not knowing you sooner?   I fear, I fear
my acquaintance with you is too short, to make
that *lasting* impression on your heart I could
wish.

SYLVANDER.

No. XV.

To Clarinda.

Sunday Night [*January* 20 ?].

THE impertinence of fools has joined with
a return of an old indisposition to make me
good for nothing to-day.   The paper has lain
before me all this evening to write to my dear
Clarinda ; but

" Fools rush'd on fools, as waves succeed to waves."

I cursed them in my soul : they sacrilegiously
disturb my meditations on her who holds my
heart.   What a creature is man !   A little alarm
last night and to-day that I am mortal, has
made such a revolution in my spirits ! there

is no philosophy, no divinity, comes half so home to the mind. I have no idea of the courage that braves Heaven. 'Tis the wild ravings of an imaginary hero in Bedlam. I can no more, Clarinda; I can scarce hold up my head; but I am happy you don't know it, you would be so uneasy.

SYLVANDER.

Monday Morning.

I am, my lovely friend, much better this morning, on the whole; but I have a horrid languor on my spirits—

"Sick of the world and all its joy,
My soul in pining sadness mourns:
Dark scenes of woe my mind employ,
The past and present in their turns."

Have you ever met with a saying of the great and likewise good Mr Locke, author of the famous "Essay on the Human Understanding"? He wrote a letter to a friend, directing it "Not to be delivered till after my decease." It ended thus:—" I know you loved me when living, and will preserve my memory now I am dead. All the use to be made of it is—that this life affords no solid satisfaction, but in the consciousness of having done well, and the hopes of another life. Adieu! I leave my best wishes with you.—J. LOCKE."

Clarinda, may I reckon on your friendship for life? I think I may. Thou Almighty Preserver of men! Thy friendship, which hitherto I have too much neglected, to secure it shall all the future days and nights of my life be my steady care! The idea of my Clarinda follows :—

> " Hide it, my heart, within that close disguise,
>   Where, mix'd with God's, her loved idea lies."

But I fear inconstancy, the consequent imperfection of human weakness. Shall I meet with a friendship that defies years of absence, and the chances and changes of fortune? Perhaps "such things are." *One* honest man I have great hopes from, that way ; but who, except a romance writer, would think on a *love* that could promise for life, in spite of distance, absence, chance, and change ; and that, too, with slender hopes of fruition? For my own part, I can say to myself in both requisitions, "Thou art the man"; I dare in cool resolve, I dare declare myself that friend and that lover. If womankind is capable of such things, Clarinda is. I trust that she is; and feel I shall be miserable if she is not. There is not one virtue which gives worth, or one sentiment which does honour to the sex, that she does not possess superior to any woman I ever saw: her exalted mind, aided a little perhaps by her situation, is, I think, capable of that nobly-romantic love-enthusiasm.

May I see you on Wednesday evening, my dear angel? The next Wednesday again will, I conjecture, be a hated day to us both. I tremble for censorious remarks for your sake; but in extraordinary cases, may not usual and useful precautions be a little dispensed with? Three evenings, three swift-winged evenings, with pinions of down, are all the past—I dare not calculate the future. I shall call at Miss Nimmo's to-morrow evening; 'twill be a farewell call.

I have written out my last sheet of paper, so I am reduced to my last half-sheet. What a strange, mysterious faculty is that thing called imagination! We have no ideas almost at all of another world; but I have often amused myself with visionary schemes of what happiness might be enjoyed by small alterations—

alterations that we can fully enter to [*sic*], in this
present state of existence.   For instance, sup-
pose you and I just as we are at present, the
same reasoning powers, sentiments, and even
desires ; the same fond curiosity for knowledge
and remarking observation in our minds—and
imagine our bodies free from pain, and the
necessary supplies for the wants of nature at
all times and easily within our reach; imagine
further that we were set free from the laws of
gravitation which bind us to this globe, and
could at pleasure fly, without inconvenience,
through all the yet unconjectured bounds of
creation—what a life of bliss should we lead
in our mutual pursuit of virtue and knowledge,
and our mutual enjoyment of friendship and
love !

I see you laughing at my fairy fancies, and
calling me a voluptuous Mahometan ; but I am
certain I should be a happy creature, beyond
anything we call bliss here below; nay, it would
be a paradise congenial to you too.   Don't you
see us hand in hand, or rather my arm about
your lovely waist, making our remarks on Sirius,
the nearest of the fixed stars ; or surveying a
comet flaming innoxious by us, as we just now

would mark the passing pomp of a travelling monarch; or in a shady bower of Mercury or Venus, dedicating the hour to love and mutual converse, relying honour, and revelling endearment—while the most exalted strains of poesy and harmony would be the ready, spontaneous language of our souls? Devotion is the favourite employment of your heart, so is it of mine; what incentives then to, and powers for reverence, gratitude, faith, and hope, in all the fervours of adoration and praise to that Being whose unsearchable wisdom, power, and goodness, so pervaded, so inspired every sense and feeling! By this time, I daresay, you will be blessing the neglect of the maid that leaves me destitute of paper.

SYLVANDER.

No. XVI.

To Clarinda.

Thursday Morning [*January* 24?].

"Unlavish Wisdom never works in vain."

I HAVE been tasking my reason, Clarinda, why a woman, who, for native genius, poignant wit, strength of mind, generous sincerity of soul, and the sweetest female tenderness, is without a peer, and whose personal charms have few, very, very few parallels among her sex ; why, or how she should fall to the blessed lot of a poor hairum-scairum poet whom Fortune had kept for her particular use, to wreak her temper on whenever she was in ill-humour. One time I conjectured that as Fortune is the most capricious jade ever known, she may have taken, not a fit of remorse, but a paroxysm of whim, to raise the poor devil out of the mire, where he had so often and so conveniently served her as a stepping-stone, and given him the most glorious boon she ever had in her gift, merely for the maggot's sake, to see how his fool head and his fool heart will bear it. At other times I was vain enough to think that Nature, who has a great deal to say with Fortune, had given the coquettish goddess some such hint as, "Here is a paragon of female ex-cellence, whose equal, in all my former com-positions, I never was lucky enough to hit on, and despair of ever doing so again ; you have cast her rather in the shades of life ; there is a certain poet of my making ; among your frolics it would not be amiss to attach him to this masterpiece of my hand, to give her that

immortality among mankind, which no woman
of any age ever more deserved, and which few
rhymesters of this age are better able to confer."

Evening, 9 *o'clock.*

I am here, absolutely so unfit to finish my
letter—pretty hearty after a bowl, which has
been constantly plied since dinner till this
moment. I have been with Mr Schetki, the
musician, and he has set the song finely. I
have no distinct ideas of anything, but that I
have drunk your health twice to-night, and that
you are all my soul holds dear in this world.

SYLVANDER.

No. XVII.

To Clarinda.

Friday [*February* 1 ?].

CLARINDA, my life, you have wounded my soul.
Can I think of your being unhappy, even though
it be not described in your pathetic elegance of
language, without being miserable? Clarinda,
can I bear to be told from you that "you will
not see me to-morrow night—that you wish the

hour of parting were come"? Do not let us impose on ourselves by sounds. . . . Why, my love, talk to me in such strong terms; every word of which cuts me to the very soul? You know, a hint, the slightest signification of your wish, is to me a sacred command.

Be reconciled, my angel, to your God, yourself, and me; and I pledge you Sylvander's honour—an oath I daresay you will trust without reserve—that you shall never more have reason to complain of his conduct. Now, my love, do not wound our next meeting with any averted looks. . . . I have marked the line of conduct—a line, I know, exactly to your taste—and which I will inviolably keep; but do not you show the least inclination to make boundaries. Seeming distrust, where you know you may confide, is a cruel sin against sensibility.

"Delicacy, you know, it was which won me to you at once: take care that you do not loosen the dearest, most sacred tie that unites us." Clarinda, I would not have stung *your* soul—I would not have bruised *your* spirit, as that harsh, crucifying "Take care," did *mine;* no, not to have gained heaven! Let me again appeal to your dear self, if Sylvander, even when he seemingly half transgressed the laws of decorum, if he did not show more chastised, trembling, faltering delicacy, than the many of the world do in keeping these laws.

O Love and Sensibility, ye have conspired against my peace! I love to madness, and I feel to torture! Clarinda, how can I forgive myself that I have ever touched a single chord in your bosom with pain! Would I do it willingly? Would any consideration, any gratification make me do so? Oh, did you love like me, you would not, you could not, deny or put off a meeting with the man who adores you; who would die a thousand deaths before he would injure you; and who must soon bid you a long farewell!

I had proposed bringing my bosom friend, Mr Ainslie, to-morrow evening, at his strong request, to see you; as he has only time to stay with us about ten minutes, for an engagement. But I shall hear from you; this afternoon, for mercy's sake!—for, till I hear from you, I am wretched. Oh, Clarinda, the tie that binds me to thee is intwisted, incorporated with my dearest threads of life!

SYLVANDER.

No. XVIII.

To Clarinda.

I WAS on my way, my love, to meet you (I never do things by halves) when I got your card. Mr Ainslie goes out of town to-morrow morning to see a brother of his, who is newly arrived from France. I am determined that he and I shall call on you together. So look you, lest I should never see to-morrow, we will call on you to-night. Mary * and you may put off tea till about seven, at which time, in the Galloway phrase, " an the beast be to the fore, and the branks bide hale," expect the humblest of your humble servants, and his dearest friend. We only propose staying half an hour—" for ought we ken." I could suffer the lash of misery eleven months in the year, were the twelfth to be composed of hours like yesternight. You are the soul of my enjoyment—all else is of the stuff of stocks and stones.

SYLVANDER.

---

* One of Mrs M'Lehose's friends.

No. XIX.

To Clarinda.

Sunday Noon.

I HAVE almost given up the Excise idea. I have been just now to wait on a great person, Miss ——'s friend ——. Why will great people not only deafen us with the din of their equipage, and dazzle us with their fastidious pomp, but they must also be so very dictatorily wise? I have been questioned like a child about my matters, and blamed and schooled for my inscription on the Stirling window. Come, Clarinda!—" Come, curse me Jacob ; come, defy me Israel!"

Sunday Night.

I have been with Miss Nimmo. She is indeed " a good soul," as my Clarinda finely says. She has reconciled me, in a good measure, to the world with her friendly prattle.

Schetki has sent me the song, set to a fine air of his composing. I have called the song " Clarinda ": I have carried it about in my pocket, and hummed it over all day.

Monday Morning.

If my prayers have any weight in heaven, this morning looks in on you and finds you in the arms of peace, except where it is charmingly interrupted by the ardours of devotion. I find so much serenity of mind, so much positive pleasure, so much fearless daring toward the world, when I warm in devotion, or feel the glorious sensation—a consciousness of Almighty friendship—that I am sure I shall soon be an honest enthusiast.

> " How are Thy servants blest, O Lord !
> How sure is their defence !
> Eternal wisdom is their guide,
> Their help Omnipotence ! "

I am, my dear Madam, yours,

SYLVANDER.

No. XX.

To Clarinda.

Sunday Morning.

I HAVE just been before the throne of my God, Clarinda; according to my association of ideas, my sentiments of love and friendship, I next devote myself to you. Yesternight I was happy—happiness that the world cannot give. I kindle at the recollection ; but it is a flame where innocence looks smiling on, and honour stands by, a sacred guard. Your heart, your fondest wishes, your dearest thoughts, these are yours to bestow : your person is unapproachable by the laws of your country ; and he loves not as I do who would make you miserable.

You are an angel, Clarinda : you are surely no mortal that "the earth owns." To kiss your hand, to live on your smile, is to me far more exquisite bliss than the dearest favours that the fairest of the sex, yourself excepted, can bestow.

Sunday Evening.

You are the constant companion of my thoughts. How wretched is the condition of one who is haunted with conscious guilt, and trembling under the idea of dreaded vengeance ! and what a placid calm, what a charming secret enjoyment it gives, to bosom the kind feelings of friendship and the formal throes of love ! Out upon the tempest of anger, the acrimonious gall of fretful impatience, the sullen frost of

F

louring resentment, or the corroding poison of withered envy! They eat up the immortal part of man. If they spent their fury only on the unfortunate objects of them, it would be something in their favour; but these miserable passions, like traitor Iscariot, betray their lord and master.

The Almighty Author of peace, and goodness, and love! do Thou give me the social heart that kindly tastes of every man's cup! Is it a draught of joy?—warm and open my heart to share it with cordial, unenvying rejoicing. Is it the bitter potion of sorrow?—melt my heart with sincerely sympathetic woe. Above all, do Thou give me the manly mind that resolutely exemplifies, in life and manners, those sentiments which I would wish to be thought to possess. The friend of my soul; there, may I never deviate from the firmest fidelity and most active kindness! Clarinda, the dear object of my fondest love; there, may the most sacred inviolate honour, the most faithful kindling constancy, ever watch and animate my every thought and imagination!

Did you ever meet with the following lines spoken of religion—your darling topic?—

" *'Tis this*, my friend, that streaks our morning bright ;
    'Tis this that gilds the horrors of our night ;
    When wealth forsakes us, and when friends are few,
    When friends are faithless, or when foes pursue ;
    'Tis this that wards the blow, or stills the smart,
    Disarms affliction, or repels its dart ;
    Within the breast bids purest rapture rise,
    Bids smiling Conscience spread her cloudless skies."

I met with these verses very early in life, and was so delighted with them, that I have them by me, copied at school.

Good night and sound rest, my dearest Clarinda !

SYLVANDER.

No. XXI.

TO CLARINDA.

Thursday Night.

I CANNOT be easy, my Clarinda, while any sentiment respecting me in your bosom gives me pain. If there is no man on earth to whom your heart and affections are justly due, it may savour of imprudence, but never of criminality, to bestow that heart and those affections where you please. The God of love meant and made those delicious attachments to be bestowed on somebody ; and even all the imprudence lies in bestowing them on an unworthy object. If this reasoning is conclusive, as it certainly is, I must be allowed to " talk of love."

It is, perhaps, rather wrong to speak highly to a friend of his letter : it is apt to lay one under a little restraint in their future letters, and restraint is the death of a friendly epistle ; but there is one passage in your last charming letter, Thomson or Shenstone never exceeded it, nor often came up to it. I shall certainly steal it, and set it in some future poetic production, and get immortal fame by it. 'Tis when you bid the scenes of nature remind me of Clarinda. Can I forget you, Clarinda ? I would detest myself as a tasteless, unfeeling, insipid, infamous blockhead. I have loved women of ordinary merit, whom I could have loved for ever. You are the first, the only unexceptionable individual of the beauteous sex that I ever met with ; and never woman more entirely possessed my soul. I know myself, and how far I can depend on passion's swell. It has been my peculiar study.

I thank you for going to Miers. Urge him, for necessity calls, to have it done by the middle of next week : Wednesday the latest day. I

want it for a breast-pin, to wear next my heart.
I propose to keep sacred set times, to wander
in the woods and wilds for meditation on you.
Then, and only then, your lovely image shall be
produced to the day, with a reverence akin to
devotion.

.　　.　　.　　.　　.　　.

To-morrow night shall not be the last.
Good night! I am perfectly stupid, as I
supped late yesternight.

SYLVANDER.

No. XXII.

TO CLARINDA.

Saturday Morning.

THERE is no time, my Clarinda, when the
conscious thrilling chords of love and friendship
give such delight, as in the pensive hours of
what our favourite Thomson calls " philosophic
melancholy." The sportive insects, who bask in
the sunshine of prosperity, or the worms, that
luxuriant crawl amid their ample wealth of
earth ; they need no Clarinda—they would
despise Sylvander, if they dared. The family of

Misfortune, a numerous group of brothers and sisters! they need a resting-place to their souls. Unnoticed, often condemned by the world—in some degree, perhaps, condemned by themselves —they feel the full enjoyment of ardent love, delicate, tender endearments, mutual esteem, and mutual reliance.

In this light I have often admired religion. In proportion as we are wrung with grief, or distracted with anxiety, the ideas of a compassionate Deity, an Almighty Protector, are doubly dear.

" 'Tis this, my friend, that streaks our morning bright ;
'Tis this that gilds the horrors of our night."

I have been this morning taking a peep through, as Young finely says, "the dark postern of time long elapsed"; and you will easily guess 'twas a rueful prospect. What a tissue of thoughtlessness, weakness, and folly! My life reminded me of a ruined temple : what strength, what proportion in some parts !—what unsightly gaps, what prostrate ruins in others! I kneeled down before the Father of Mercies, and said, "Father, I have sinned against Heaven, and in Thy sight, and am no more worthy to be called Thy son!" I rose, eased and strengthened. I despise the superstition of a fanatic, but I love the religion of a man. "The future," said I to myself, "is still before me : there let me

> ' On reason build resolve—
> That column of true majesty in man ! '

I have difficulties many to encounter," said I ; " but they are not absolutely insuperable : and where is firmness of mind shown, but in exertion ? Mere declamation is bombast rant. Besides, wherever I am, or in whatever situation I may be—

> ''Tis nought to me,
> Since God is ever present, ever felt,
> In the void waste as in the city full ;
> And where He vital breathes, there must be joy.'"

Saturday Night, Half after Ten.

What luxury of bliss I was enjoying at this time yesternight! My ever dearest Clarinda, you have stolen away my soul : but you have refined, you have exalted it ; you have given it a stronger sense of virtue, and a stronger relish for piety. Clarinda, first of your sex ! if ever I am the veriest wretch on earth to forget you—

if ever your lovely image is effaced from my soul—

" May I be lost, no eye to weep my end,
 And find no earth that's base enough to bury me ! "

What trifling silliness is the childish fondness of the every-day children of the world! 'Tis the unmeaning toying of the younglings of the fields and forests; but, where sentiment and fancy unite their sweets, where taste and delicacy refine, where wit adds the flavour, and good sense gives strength and spirit to all, what a delicious draught is the hour of tender endearment !

No. XXIII.

To Clarinda.

. . . I am a discontented ghost, a perturbed spirit. Clarinda, if you ever forget Sylvander, may you be happy, but he will be miserable.

Oh, what a fool I am in love! what an extravagant prodigal of affection! Why are your sex called the tender sex, when I never have met with one who can repay me in passion? They are either not so rich in love as I am, or they are niggards where I am lavish.

O Thou, whose I am, and whose are all my
ways! Thou see'st me here, the hapless wreck
of tides and tempests in my own bosom : do
Thou direct to Thyself that ardent love, for
which I have so often sought a return in vain
from my fellow-creatures! If Thy goodness
has yet such a gift in store for me as an equal
return of affection from her who, Thou knowest,
is dearer to me than life, do Thou bless and
hallow our band of love and friendship ; watch
over us, in all our outgoings and incomings for
good ; and may the tie that unites our hearts be
strong and indissoluble as the thread of man's
immortal life !

I am just going to take your blackbird, the
sweetest, I am sure, that ever sung, and prune
its wings a little.

SYLVANDER.

No. XXIV.

TO CLARINDA.

Tuesday Morning.

I CANNOT go out to-day, my dearest love,
without sending you half a line by way of a sin-

offering; but, believe me, 'twas the sin of ignorance. Could you think that I intended to hurt you by anything I said yesternight? Nature has been too kind to you for your happiness, your delicacy, your sensibility. Oh why should such glorious qualifications be the fruitful source of woe! You have "murdered sleep" to me last night. I went to bed impressed with an idea that you were unhappy; and every start I closed my eyes, busy Fancy painted you in such scenes of romantic misery, that I would almost be persuaded you are not well this morning.

> " If I unwitting have offended,
> Impute it not."
> " But while we live
> But one short hour, perhaps, between us two
> Let there be peace."

If Mary has not gone by the time this reaches you, give her my best compliments. She is a charming girl, and highly worthy of the noblest love.

I send you a poem to read till I call on you this night, which will be about nine. I wish I could procure some potent spell, some fairy charm, that would protect from injury, or restore to rest, that bosom chord, "trembling alive all o'er," on which hangs your peace of mind. I thought, vainly I fear thought, that the devotion of love—love strong as even you can feel, love guarded, invulnerably guarded, by all the purity of virtue, and all the pride of honour—I thought such a love might make you happy. Shall I be mistaken? I can no more, for hurry.

No. XXV.

To Clarinda.

Friday Morning, 7 o'clock.

Your fears for Mary are truly laughable. I suppose, my love, you and I showed her a scene which, perhaps, made her wish that she had a swain, and one who could love like me ; and 'tis a thousand pities that so good a heart as hers should want an aim, an object. I am miserably stupid this morning. Yesterday I dined with a baronet, and sat pretty late over the bottle. And "who hath woe—who hath sorrow? they that tarry long at the wine ; they that go to seek mixed wine." Forgive me, likewise, a quotation from my favourite author.

Solomon's knowledge of the world is very great. He may be looked on as the *Spectator* or *Adventurer* of his day: and it is, indeed, surprising what a sameness has ever been in human nature. The broken, but strongly characterising hints, that the royal author gives us of the manners of the court of Jerusalem and country of Israel are, in their great outlines, the same pictures that London and England, Versailles and France, exhibit some three thousand years later. The loves in the " Song of Songs " are all in the spirit of Lady M. W. Montagu, or Madame Ninon de l'Enclos; though, for my part, I dislike both the ancient and modern voluptuaries ; and will dare to affirm, that such an attachment as mine to Clarinda, and such evenings as she and I have spent, are what these greatly respectable and deeply experienced judges of life and love never dreamed of.

I shall be with you this evening between eight and nine, and shall keep as sober hours as you could wish.

I am ever, my dear Madam, yours,

SYLVANDER.

No. XXVI.

To Clarinda.

My ever dearest Clarinda,

I make a numerous dinner-party wait me while I read yours and write this. Do not require that I should cease to love you, to adore you in my soul; 'tis to me impossible: your peace and happiness are to me dearer than my soul. Name the terms on which you wish to see me, to correspond with me, and you have them. I must love, pine, mourn, and adore in secret: this you must not deny me. You will ever be to me

> " Dear as the light that visits those sad eyes,
> Dear as the ruddy drops that warm my heart."

I have not patience to read the Puritanic scrawl. Damned sophistry! Ye heavens, Thou God of nature, Thou Redeemer of mankind! ye look down with approving eyes on a passion inspired by the purest flame, and guarded by truth, delicacy, and honour; but the half-inch soul of an unfeeling, cold-blooded, pitiful Presbyterian bigot cannot forgive anything above his dungeon-bosom and foggy head.

Farewell! I'll be with you to-morrow evening; and be at rest in your mind. I will be yours in the way you think most to your happiness. I dare not proceed. I love, and will love you; and will, with joyous confidence, approach the throne of the Almighty Judge of men with your dear idea; and will despise the scum of sentiment and the mist of sophistry. .

SYLVANDER.

No. XXVII.

TO CLARINDA.

Wednesday, Midnight.

MADAM,

After a wretched day, I am preparing for a sleepless night. I am going to address myself to the Almighty Witness of my actions—some time, perhaps very soon, my Almighty Judge. I am not going to be the advocate of Passion: be Thou my inspirer and testimony, O God, as I plead the cause of truth!

I have read over your friend's haughty, dictatorial letter: you are only answerable to your God in such a matter. Who gave any fellow-creature of yours (a fellow-creature incapable of being your judge, because not your peer) a right to catechise, scold, undervalue, abuse, and insult, wantonly and inhumanly to insult, you thus? I don't wish, not even wish, to deceive you, Madam. The Searcher of hearts is my witness how dear you are to me; but though it were possible you could be still dearer to me, I would not even kiss your hand at the expense of your conscience. Away with declamation! let us appeal to the bar of common sense. It is not mouthing everything sacred; it is not vague ranting assertions; it is not assuming, haughtily and insultingly assuming, the dictatorial language of a Roman pontiff, that must dissolve a union like ours. Tell me, Madam, are you under the least shadow of an obligation to bestow your love, tenderness, caresses, affections, heart and soul, on Mr M'Lehose—the man who has repeatedly, habitually, and barbarously broken through every tie of duty, nature, or gratitude to you? The laws of your country, indeed, for the most useful reasons of policy and sound government, have made your person inviolate; but are your heart and affections bound to one who gives not the least return of either to you? You cannot do it; it is not in the nature of things that you are bound to do it; the common feelings of humanity forbid it. Have you, then, a heart and affections which are no man's right? You have. It would be highly, ridiculously absurd to suppose the contrary. Tell me, then, in the name of common sense, can it be wrong, is such a supposition compatible with the plainest ideas of right and wrong, that it is improper to bestow the heart and these affections on another—while that bestowing is not in the smallest degree hurtful to your duty to God, to your children, to yourself, or to society at large?

This is the great test; the consequences: let us see them. In a widowed, forlorn, lonely situation, with a bosom glowing with love and tenderness, yet so delicately situated that you cannot indulge these nobler feelings except you meet with a man who has a soul capable . . .

No. XXVIII.

To Clarinda.

"I am distressed for thee, my brother Jonathan." I have suffered, Clarinda, from your letter. My soul was in arms at the sad perusal. I dreaded that I had acted wrong. If I have wronged you, God forgive me. But, Clarinda, be comforted. Let us raise the tone of our feelings a little higher and bolder. A fellow-creature who leaves us—who spurns us without just cause, though once our bosom friend—up with a little honest pride: let him go! How shall I comfort you, who am the cause of the injury? Can I wish that I had never seen you —that we had never met? No, I never will. But, have I thrown you friendless?—there is almost distraction in the thought. Father of Mercies! against Thee often have I sinned: through Thy grace I will endeavour to do so no more. She who, Thou knowest, is dearer to me than myself—pour Thou the balm of peace into her past wounds, and hedge her about with Thy peculiar care, all her future days and nights. Strengthen her tender, noble mind firmly to suffer and magnanimously to bear. Make me worthy of that friendship, that love she honours me with. May my attachment to her be pure as devotion, and lasting as immortal life! O Almighty Goodness, hear me! Be to her at all times, particularly in the hour of

G

distress or trial, a friend and comforter, a guide and guard.

> " How are Thy servants blest, O Lord,
>   How sure is their defence !
>   Eternal wisdom is their guide,
>   Their help Omnipotence."

Forgive me, Clarinda, the injury I have done you. To-night I shall be with you, as indeed I shall be ill at ease till I see you.

SYLVANDER.

No. XXIX.

To Clarinda.

Two o'clock.

I JUST now received your first letter of yesterday, by the careless negligence of the penny-post. Clarinda, matters are grown very serious with us; then seriously hear me, and hear me, Heaven—I met you, my dear . . . , by far the first of womankind, at least to me; I esteemed, I loved you at first sight; the longer I am acquainted with you, the more innate amiableness and worth I discover in you. You have suffered a loss, I confess, for my sake: but if the firmest, steadiest, warmest friendship—if every endeavour to be worthy of your friendship—if a love, strong as the ties of nature, and holy as the duties of religion—if all these can make anything like a compensation for the evil I have occasioned you, if they be worth your acceptance, or can in the least add to your enjoyments—so help Sylvander, ye Powers above, in his hour of need, as he freely gives these all to Clarinda !

I esteem you, I love you as a friend : I admire you, I love you as a woman beyond any one in all the circle of creation ; I know I shall continue to esteem you, to love you, to pray for you—nay, to pray for myself for your sake.

Expect me at eight—and believe me to be ever, my dearest Madam,

Yours most entirely,

Sylvander.

No. XXX.

To Clarinda.

When matters, my love, are desperate, we must put on a desperate face—

" On reason build resolve,
That column of true majesty in man "—

or, as the same author finely says in another
place—

> " Let thy soul spring up
> And lay strong hold for help on Him that made thee."

I am yours, Clarinda, for life. Never be dis-
couraged at all this. Look forward : in a few
weeks I shall be somewhere or other, out of the
possibility of seeing you ; till then, I shall write
you often, but visit you seldom. Your fame,
your welfare, your happiness, are dearer to me
than any gratification whatever. Be comforted,
my love! the present moment is the worst ; the
lenient hand of time is daily and hourly either
lightening the burden, or making us insensible
to the weight. None of these friends—I mean
Mr —— and the other gentleman—can hurt
your worldly support ; and of their friendship,
in a little time you will learn to be easy, and
by-and-by to be happy without it. A decent
means of livelihood in the world, an approving
God, a peaceful conscience, and one firm trusty
friend—can anybody that has these be said to
be unhappy ? These are yours.

To-morrow evening I shall be with you about
eight, probably for the last time till I return to

Edinburgh. In the meantime, should any of these two unlucky friends question you respecting me, whether I am *the man*, I do not think they are entitled to any information. As to their jealousy and spying, I despise them. Adieu, my dearest Madam!

SYLVANDER.

No. XXXI.

TO CLARINDA.

GLASGOW, *Monday Evening, Nine o'clock.*

THE attraction of love, I find, is in an inverse proportion to the attraction of the Newtonian philosophy. In the system of Sir Isaac, the nearer objects were to one another, the stronger was the attractive force. In my system, every milestone that marked my progress from Clarinda, awakened a keener pang of attachment to her. How do you feel, my love? Is your heart ill at ease? I fear it. God forbid that these persecutors should harass that peace, which is more precious to me than my own. Be assured I shall ever think on you, muse on you, and in my moments of devotion, pray for you. The hour that you are not in my thoughts, "be that hour darkness; let the shadows of death cover it; let it not be numbered in the hours of the day!"

> "When I forget the darling theme,
> Be my tongue mute! my fancy paint no more!
> And, dead to joy, forget my heart to beat!"

I have just met with my old friend, the ship captain *—guess my pleasure: to meet you could alone have given me more. My brother William, too, the young saddler, has come to Glasgow to meet me; and here are we three spending the evening.

I arrived here too late to write by post; but I'll wrap half-a-dozen sheets of blank paper together, and send it by the Fly, under the name of a parcel. You will hear from me next post-town. I would write you a longer letter, but for the present circumstances of my friend.

Adieu, my Clarinda! I am just going to propose your health by way of grace drink.

SYLVANDER.

---

* Mr Richard Brown.

No. XXXII.

To Clarinda.

KILMARNOCK, *Friday* [*Feb.* 22].

I WROTE you, my dear Madam, the moment I alighted in Glasgow. Since then I have not had opportunity; for in Paisley, where I arrived next day, my worthy, wise friend Mr Pattison did not allow me a moment's respite. I was there ten hours; during which time I was introduced to nine men worth six thousands; five men worth ten thousands; his brother, richly worth twenty thousands; and a young weaver, who will have thirty thousands good when his father, who has no more children than the said weaver, and a Whig kirk, dies. Mr P. was bred a zealous Anti-burgher; but during his widowerhood he has found their strictness incompatible with certain compromises he is often obliged to make with those powers of darkness—the devil, the world, and the flesh. . . . His only daughter, who, "if the beast be to the fore, and the branks bide hale," will have seven thousand pounds when her old father steps into the dark factory-office of eternity with his well-thrummed

web of life, has put him again and again in a
commendable fit of indignation by requesting
a harpsichord. "O these boarding-schools!"
exclaims my prudent friend: "she was a good
spinner and sewer till I was advised by her foes
and mine to give her a year of Edinburgh!"

After two bottles more, my much-respected
friend opened up to me a project—a legitimate
child of Wisdom and Good Sense: 'twas no
less than a long-thought-on and deeply-matured
design, to marry a girl fully as elegant in her
form as the famous priestess whom Saul con-
sulted in his last hours, and who had been
second maid of honour to his deceased wife.
This, you may be sure, I highly applauded; so
I hope for a pair of gloves by-and-by. I spent
the two bypast days at Dunlop House, with
that worthy family to whom I was deeply in-
debted early in my poetic career; and in about
two hours I shall present your "twa wee sarkies"
to the little fellow. My dearest Clarinda, you
are ever present with me; and these hours,
that drawl by among the fools and rascals of
this world, are only supportable in the idea,
that they are the forerunners of that happy
hour that ushers me to "the mistress of my

soul." Next week I shall visit Dumfries, and next again return to Edinburgh. My letters, in these hurrying dissipated hours, will be heavy trash ; but you know the writer. God bless you !

SYLVANDER.

No. XXXIII.

To Clarinda.

CUMNOCK [*Sunday*], *March* 2, 1788.

I HOPE, and am certain, that my generous Clarinda will not think my silence, for now a long week, has been in any degree owing to my forgetfulness. I have been tossed about through the country ever since I wrote you ; and am here, returning from Dumfriesshire, at an inn, the post-office of the place, with just so long time as my horse eats his corn, to write you. I have been hurried with business and dissipation almost equal to the insidious decree of the Persian monarch's mandate, when he forbade asking petition of God or man for forty days. Had the venerable prophet been as throng [busy] as I, he had not broken the decree, at least not thrice a-day.

I am thinking my farming scheme will yet hold. A worthy, intelligent farmer, my father's friend and my own, has been with me on the spot: he thinks the bargain practicable. I am myself, on a more serious review of the lands, much better pleased with them. I won't mention this in writing to anybody but you and [Ainslie]. Don't accuse me of being fickle: I have the two plans of life before me, and I wish to adopt the one most likely to procure me independence. I shall be in Edinburgh next week. I long to see you: your image is omnipresent to me; nay, I am convinced I would soon idolatrize it most seriously—so much do absence and memory improve the medium through which one sees the much-loved object. To-night, at the sacred hour of eight, I expect to meet you—at the Throne of Grace. I hope, as I go home to-night, to find a letter from you at the post-office in Mauchline. I have just once seen that dear hand since I left Edinburgh—a letter indeed which much affected me. Tell me, first of woman-kind! will my warmest attachment, my sincerest friendship, my correspondence—will they be any compensation for the sacrifices you make for my sake? If they will, they are yours. If I settle

on the farm I propose, I am just a day and a
half's ride from Edinburgh. We will meet—
don't you say "perhaps too often!"

Farewell, my fair, my charming poetess! May
all good things ever attend you!

I am ever, my dearest Madam, yours,

SYLVANDER.

No. XXXIV.

SYLVANDER TO CLARINDA.

[*March* 6, 1788.]

I OWN myself guilty, Clarinda: I should
have written you last week. But when you
recollect, my dearest Madam, that yours of this
night's post is only the third I have from you,
and that this is the fifth or sixth I have sent
to you, you will not reproach me, with a good
grace, for unkindness. I have always some kind
of idea not to sit down to write a letter, except
I have time, and possession of my faculties, so
as to do some justice to my letter; which at
present is rarely my situation. For instance,
yesterday I dined at a friend's at some distance:

the savage hospitality of this country spent me the most part of the night over the nauseous potion in the bowl. This day—sick—headache —low spirits—miserable—fasting, except for a draught of water or small beer. Now eight o'clock at night; only able to crawl ten minutes' walk into Mauchline, to wait the post, in the pleasurable hope of hearing from the mistress of my soul.

But truce with all this! When I sit down to write to you, all is happiness and peace. A hundred times a day do I figure you before your taper, your book or work laid aside as I get within the room. How happy have I been! and how little of that scantling portion of time, called the life of man, is sacred to happiness, much less transport.

I could moralize to-night like a death's-head.

> " Oh what is life, that thoughtless wish of all !
> A drop of honey in a draught of gall."

Nothing astonishes me more, when a little sickness clogs the wheels of life, than the thoughtless career we run in the hour of health. " None saith, Where is God, my Maker, that giveth songs in the night: who teacheth us more knowledge than the beasts of the field, and more understanding than the fowls of the air ? "

Give me, my Maker, to remember Thee ! Give me to act up to the dignity of my nature ! Give me to feel "another's woe"; and continue with me that dear loved friend that feels with mine !

The dignifying and dignified consciousness of an honest man, and the well-grounded trust in approving Heaven, are two most substantial foundations of happiness. . . .

I could not have written a page to any mortal except yourself. I'll write you by Sunday's post. Adieu ! Good night !

SYLVANDER.

No. XXXV.

SYLVANDER TO CLARINDA.

MOSSGIEL, *March* 7, 1788.

CLARINDA, I have been so stung with your reproach for unkindness—a sin so unlike me, a sin I detest more than a breach of the whole

Decalogue, fifth, sixth, seventh, and ninth articles excepted—that I believe I shall not rest in my grave about it, if I die before I see you. You have often allowed me the head to judge and the heart to feel the influence of female excellence : was it not blasphemy then, against your own charms and against my feelings, to suppose that a short fortnight could abate my passion ?

You, my love, may have your cares and anxieties to disturb you ; but they are the usual occurrences of life. Your future views are fixed, and your mind in a settled routine. Could not you, my ever dearest Madam, make a little allowance for a man, after long absence, paying a short visit to a country full of friends, relations, and early intimates ? Cannot you guess, my Clarinda, what thoughts, what cares, what anxious forebodings, hopes, and fears, must crowd the breast of the man of keen sensibility, when no less is on the *tapis* than his aim, his employment, his very existence through future life ?

To be overtopped in anything else, I can bear ; but in the tests of generous love, I defy all mankind ! not even to the tender, the fond, the loving Clarinda ; she whose strength of attachment, whose melting soul, may vie with Eloise and Sappho ; not even she can overpay the affection she owes me !

Now that, not my apology, but my defence is made, I feel my soul respire more easily. I know you will go along with me in my justification : would to Heaven you could in my adoption, too! I mean an adoption beneath the stars—an adoption where I might revel in the immediate beams of

"She the bright sun of all her sex."

I would not have you, my dear Madam, so much hurt at Miss Nimmo's coldness. 'Tis placing yourself below her, an honour she by no means deserves. We ought, when we wish to be economists in happiness—we ought, in the first place, to fix the standard of our own character; and when, on full examination, we know where we stand, and how much ground we occupy, let us contend for it as property ; and those who seem to doubt or deny us what is justly ours, let us either pity their prejudices or despise their judgment. I know, my dear, you will say this is self-conceit ; but I call it

self-knowledge: the one is the overweening
opinion of a fool, who fancies himself to be
what he wishes himself to be thought; the
other is the honest justice that a man of sense,
who has thoroughly examined the subject, owes
to himself. Without this standard, this column
in our own mind, we are perpetually at the
mercy of the petulance, the mistakes, the pre-
judices, nay, the very weakness and wickedness
of our fellow-creatures.

I urge this, my dear, both to confirm myself
in the doctrine which, I assure you, I sometimes
need, and because I know that this causes you
often much disquiet. To return to Miss Nimmo.
She is most certainly a worthy soul; and
equalled by very, very few in goodness of heart.
But can she boast more goodness of heart than
Clarinda? Not even prejudice will dare to say
so. For penetration and discernment, Clarinda
sees far beyond her. To wit, Miss Nimmo dare
make no pretence: to Clarinda's wit, scarce any
of her sex dare make pretence. Personal
charms, it would be ridiculous to run the
parallel: and for conduct in life, Miss Nimmo
was never called out, either much to do, or to
suffer. Clarinda has been both; and has per-

formed her part, where Miss Nimmo would have sunk at the bare idea.

Away, then, with these disquietudes! Let us pray with the honest weaver of Kilbarchan, "Lord, send us a gude conceit o' oursel'!" or in the words of the auld sang—

> " Who does me disdain, I can scorn them again,
>   And I'll never mind any such foes."

There is an error in the commerce of intimacy. . . .

Happy is our lot, indeed, when we meet with an honest merchant, who is qualified to deal with us on our own terms; but that is a rarity: with almost everybody we must pocket our pearls, less or more, and learn, in the old Scots phrase, "To gie sic like as we get." For this reason we should try to erect a kind of bank or storehouse in our own mind; or, as the Psalmist says, "We should commune with our own hearts and be still." . . .

I wrote you yesternight, which will reach you long before this can. I may write Mr Ainslie before I see him, but I am not sure.

Farewell! and remember

SYLVANDER.

II

No. XXXVI.

SYLVANDER TO CLARINDA.

Monday Noon [*March* 17].

I WILL meet you to-morrow, Clarinda, as you appoint. My Excise affair is just concluded, and I have got my order for instructions : so far good. Wednesday night I am engaged to sup among some of the principals of the Excise, so can only make a call for you that evening ; but next day, I stay to dine with one of the Commissioners, so cannot go till Friday morning.

Your hopes, your fears, your cares, my love, are mine ; so don't mind them. I will take you in my hand through the dreary wilds of this world, and scare away the ravening bird or beast that would annoy you. I saw Mary in town to-day, and asked her if she had seen you. I shall certainly bespeak Mr Ainslie, as you desire.

Excuse me, my dearest angel, this hurried scrawl and miserable paper ; circumstances make both. Farewell till to-morrow.

SYLVANDER.

No. XXXVII.

SYLVANDER TO CLARINDA.

Tuesday Morning [*March* 18].

I AM just hurrying away to wait on the Great Man, Clarinda ; but I have more respect to my own peace and happiness than to set out without waiting on you ; for my imagination, like a child's favourite bird, will fondly flutter along with this scrawl, till it perch on your bosom. I thank you for all the happiness you bestowed on me yesterday. The walk—delightful ; the evening — rapture. Do not be uneasy to-day, Clarinda ; forgive me. I am in rather better spirits to-day, though I had but an indifferent night. Care, anxiety sat on my spirits ; and all the cheerfulness of this morning is the fruit of some serious, important ideas that lie, in their realities, beyond " the dark and the narrow house," as Ossian, prince of poets, says. The Father of Mercies be with you, Clarinda ! and every good thing attend you !

SYLVANDER.

No. XXXVIII.

Sylvander to Clarinda.

Wednesday Morning [*March* 19].

CLARINDA, will that envious night-cap hinder you from appearing at the window as I pass? "Who is she that looketh forth as the morning; fair as the sun, clear as the moon, terrible as an army with banners?"

Do not accuse me of fond folly for this line; you know I am a cool lover. I mean by these presents greeting, to let you to wit, that arch-rascal Creech has not done my business yester-night, which has put off my leaving town till Monday morning. To-morrow at eleven I meet with him for the last time; just the hour I should have met far more agreeable company.

You will tell me this evening whether you cannot make our hour of meeting to-morrow one o'clock. I have just now written Creech such a letter, that the very goose-feather in my hand shrunk back from the line, and seemed to say, "I exceedingly fear and quake!" I am forming ideal schemes of vengeance. . . . Adieu, and think on

SYLVANDER.

No. XXXIX.

Sylvander to Clarinda.

Friday, Nine o'clock, Night [*March* 21].

I AM just now come in, and have read your letter. The first thing I did was to thank the divine Disposer of events, that He has had such happiness in store for me as the connexion I have with you. Life, my Clarinda, is a weary, barren path; and woe be to him or her that ventures on it alone! For me, I have my dearest partner of my soul: Clarinda and I will make out our pilgrimage together. Wherever I am, I shall constantly let her know how I go on, what I observe in the world around me, and what adventures I meet with. Will it please you, my love, to get every week, or at least every fortnight, a packet, two or three sheets, full of remarks, nonsense, news, rhymes, and old songs? Will you open, with satisfaction and delight, a letter from a man who loves you, who has loved you, and who will love you to death, through death, and for ever? Oh, Clarinda! what do I owe to Heaven for blessing me with such a piece of exalted excellence as you! I call over your idea, as a miser counts over his treasure. Tell me, were you studious to please me last night? I am sure you did it to transport. How rich am I who have such a treasure as you! You know me; you know how to make me happy; and you do it most effectually. God bless you with

"Long life, long youth, long pleasure, and a friend !"

To-morrow night, according to your own direction, I shall watch the window : 'tis the star that guides me to paradise. The great relish to all is, that Honour, that Innocence, that Religion, are the witnesses and guarantees of our happiness. "The Lord God knoweth," and perhaps "Israel he shall know," my love and your merit. Adieu, Clarinda ! I am going to remember you in my prayers.

SYLVANDER.

No. XL.

TO CLARINDA.

MADAM,   *March 9, 1789.*

The letter you wrote me to Heron's carried its own answer in its bosom; you forbade me to write you, unless I was willing to plead guilty to a certain indictment that you were pleased to bring against me. As I am convinced of my own innocence, and though conscious of high imprudence and egregious folly, can lay my hand on my breast and attest the rectitude of my heart, you will pardon me, Madam, if I do not carry my complaisance so far as humbly to acquiesce in the name of villain, merely out of compliment to your opinion, much as I esteem your judgment, and warmly as I regard your worth.

I have already told you, and I again aver it, that at the period of time alluded to I was not under the smallest moral tie to Mrs Burns; nor did I, nor could I, then know all the powerful circumstances that omnipotent necessity was busy laying in wait for me. When you call over the scenes that have passed between us, you will survey the conduct of an honest man, struggling successfully with temptations the most powerful that ever beset humanity, and preserving untainted honour in situations where the austerest virtue would have forgiven a fall; situations that, I will dare to say, not a single individual of all his kind, even with half his sensibility and passion, could have encountered without ruin; and I leave you to guess, Madam, how such a man is likely to digest an accusation of perfidious treachery.

Was I to blame, Madam, in being the distracted victim of charms which, I affirm it, no man ever approached with impunity? Had I seen the least glimmering of hope that these charms could ever have been mine, or even had not iron necessity — but these are unavailing words.

I would have called on you when I was in town—indeed, I could not have resisted it—but that Mr Ainslie told me that you were determined to avoid your windows while I was in town, lest even a glance of me should occur in the street.

When I have regained your good opinion, perhaps I may venture to solicit your friendship; but, be that as it may, the first of her sex I ever knew shall always be the object of my warmest good wishes.   R. B.

No. XLI.

SYLVANDER TO CLARINDA.

February 1790 (?).

I HAVE indeed been ill, Madam, the whole winter. An incessant headache, depression of spirits, and all the truly miserable consequences of a deranged nervous system, have made dreadful havoc of my health and peace. Add to all this a line of life into which I have lately entered obliges me to ride, on the average, at least 200 miles every week. However, thank Heaven, I am now greatly better in my health. . . .

I cannot, will not, enter into extenuatory circumstances; else I could show you how my precipitate, headlong, unthinking conduct leagued with a conjuncture of unlucky events to thrust me out of a possibility of keeping the path of rectitude to curse me, by an irreconcilable war between my duty and my nearest wishes, and to damn me with a choice only of different species of error and misconduct.

I dare not trust myself further with this subject. The following song is one of my latest productions, and I send it you as I would do anything else, because it pleases myself.

[Here follows " My Lovely Nancy."]

No. XLII.

SYLVANDER TO CLARINDA.

[Burns had been to Edinburgh at the end of November and beginning of December, and had there seen Mrs M'Lehose. She had resolved to go to her worthless but repentant husband in Jamaica, and sailed in February 1792.]

I HAVE received both your last letters, Madam, and ought and would have answered the first long ago. But on what subject shall I write you? How can you expect a correspondent should write you when you declare that you mean to preserve his letters, with a view, sooner or later, to expose them in the pillory of derision and the rock of criticism? This is gagging me completely as to speaking the sentiments of my bosom; else, Madam, I could perhaps too truly

" Join grief with grief, and echo sighs to thine ! "

I have perused your most beautiful but most pathetic poem; do not ask me how often or with what emotions. You know that " I dare to *sin*, but not to *lie*." Your verses wring the confession from my inmost soul, that—I will say it, expose it if you please—that I have more than once in my life been the victim of a damning conjuncture of circumstances; and that to see you must be ever

"Dear as the light that visits these sad eyes."

I have just, since I had yours, composed the following stanzas. Let me know your opinion of them.

[Here are transcribed the lines beginning, "Sweet Sensibility, how charming," &c.]

No. XLIII.

To Clarinda.

[Enclosing the "Lament of Mary, Queen of Scots," Burns wrote as follows :—]

LEADHILLS, *Thursday Noon* [*Dec.* 11, 1791].

SUCH, my dearest Clarinda, were the words of the amiable but unfortunate Mary. Misfortune seems to take a peculiar pleasure in darting her arrows against "honest men and bonnie lasses." Of this you are too, too just a proof; but may your future be a bright exception to the remark. In the words of Hamlet—

"Adieu, adieu, adieu! Remember me."

SYLVANDER.

No. XLIV.

To Clarinda.

DUMFRIES [*December* 15 (?), 1791].

I HAVE some merit, my ever dearest of women, in attracting and securing the honest heart of Clarinda. In her I meet with the most accomplished of all womankind, the first of all God's works, and yet I, even I, have the good fortune to appear amiable in her sight.

By the by, this is the sixth letter that I have written since I left you ; and if you were an ordinary being, as you are a creature very extraordinary—an instance of what God Almighty, in the plenitude of His power and the fulness of His goodness, can make !—I would never forgive you for not answering my letters.

I have sent your hair, a part of the parcel you gave me, with a measure, to Mr Brice, the jeweller, to get a ring done for me. I have likewise sent in the verses " On Sensibility," altered to—

> " Sensibility, how charming,
> Dearest Nancy, thou can tell," &c.,

to the editor of " Scots Songs," of which you

have three volumes, to set to a most beautiful
air—out of compliment to the first of women,
my ever-beloved, my ever-sacred Clarinda. I
shall probably write you to-morrow. In the
meantime, from a man who is literally drunk
accept and forgive!

R. B.

No. XLV.

To Clarinda.

I SUPPOSE, my dear Madam, that by your
neglecting to inform me of your arrival in
Europe—a circumstance that could not be in-
different to me, as indeed no occurrence relating
to you can—you meant to leave me to guess
and gather that a correspondence I once had
the honour and felicity to enjoy is to be no
more. Alas! what heavy-laden sounds are
these—"No more!" The wretch who has never
tasted pleasure has never known woe: what
drives the soul to madness is the recollection
of joys that are "no more!" But this is not
language to the world: they do not understand
it. But come, ye few—the children of feeling
and sentiment!—ye whose trembling bosom-
chords ache to unutterable anguish as recol-

lection gushes on the heart!—ye who are capable of an attachment keen as the arrows of Death, and strong as the vigour of immortal being—come! and your ears shall drink a tale— But hush! I must not, cannot, tell it; agony is in the recollection, and frenzy in the recital!

But, Madam, to leave the paths that lead to madness, I congratulate your friends on your return; and I hope that the precious health, which Miss P. tells me is so much injured, is restored or restoring. . . .

I present you a book: may I hope you will accept it? I daresay you will have brought your books with you. The fourth vol. of the "Scots Songs" is published. [*August* 1792.] I will presume to send it you. Shall I hear from you? But first hear me. No cold language —no prudential documents: I despise advice and scorn control. If you are not to write such language, such sentiments, as you know I shall wish, shall delight to receive, I conjure you, by wounded pride, by ruined peace, by frantic dis- appointed passion, by all the many ills that constitute that sum of human woes, a broken heart!!! to me be silent for ever. . . .

R. B.

No. XLVI.

To Clarinda.

BEFORE you ask me why I have not written you, first let me be informed by you, *how* I shall write you? "In friendship," you say; and I have many a time taken up my pen to try an epistle of "friendship" to you, but it will not do; 'tis like Jove grasping a popgun after having wielded his thunder. When I take up the pen, recollection ruins me. Ah, my ever-dearest Clarinda! Clarinda! What a host of memory's tenderest offspring crowd on my fancy at that sound! But I must not indulge that subject; you have forbid it.

I am extremely happy to learn that your precious health is re-established, and that you are once more fit to enjoy that satisfaction in existence which health alone can give us. My old friend Ainslie has indeed been kind to you. Tell him, that I envy him the power of serving you. I had a letter from him a while ago, but it was so dry, so distant, so like a card to one of his clients, that I could scarce bear to read it, and have not yet answered it. He is a good, honest fellow, and *can* write a friendly letter, which would do equal honour to his head and his heart, as a whole sheaf of his letters which I have by me will witness; and though Fame does not blow her trumpet at my approach *now* as she did *then*, when he first honoured me with his friendship, yet I am as proud as ever; and when I am laid in my grave, I wish to be stretched at my full length, that I may occupy every inch of ground I have a right to.

You would laugh were you to see me where I am just now. Would to Heaven you were here to laugh with me, though I am afraid that crying would be our first employment! Here am I set, a solitary hermit, in the solitary room of a solitary inn, with a solitary bottle of wine by me, as grave and as stupid as an owl, but, like that owl, still faithful to my old song; in confirmation of which, my dear Mrs Mac, here is your good health! May the hand-waled benisons o' Heaven bless your bonnie face; and the wratch wha skellies at your welfare, may the auld tinkler deil get him, to clout his rotten heart! Amen.

You must know, my dearest Madam, that these now many years, wherever I am, in whatever company, when a married lady is called as a toast, I constantly give you; but as your name has never passed my lips, even to my most intimate friend, I give you by the name of Mrs Mac. This is so well known among my acquaintances, that when any married lady is called for, the toast-master will say: " Oh, we need not ask him who it is: here's Mrs Mack! " I have also, among my convivial friends, set on foot a round of toasts, which I call a round of Arcadian Shepherdesses—that is, a round of favourite ladies, under female names celebrated in ancient song; and then you are my Clarinda. So, my lovely Clarinda, I devote this glass of wine to a most ardent wish for your happiness.

In vain would Prudence, with decorous sneer,
Point out a censuring world, and bid me fear:
Above that world on wings of love I rise;
I know its worst, and can that worst despise.

" Wronged, injured, shunned, unpitied, unredrest—
The mocked quotation of the scorner's jest "—
Let Prudence' direst bodements on me fall,
Clarinda, rich reward! o'erpays them all.

I have been rhyming a little of late, but I do not know if they are worth postage.

I

Tell me what you think of the following monody.

The subject of the foregoing is a woman of fashion in this country,* with whom at one period I was well acquainted. By some scandalous conduct to me, and two or three other gentlemen here as well as me, she steered so far to the north of my good opinion, that I have made her the theme of several ill-natured things. . . .

R. B.

---

* Mrs Riddel.

NOTES ON CLARINDA
AND HER CORRESPONDENCE.

Notes on the
Clarinda Correspondence.

By JOHN MUIR, F.S.A. Scot.

———

IN the letter with which he opens his celebrated correspondence with Clarinda, Burns mentions some lines of his which he commends in a style so unwonted when speaking of his own work, that we cannot but regret that they have not been preserved. He writes, December 3, 1787 :—

"Our worthy friend, in her usual pleasant way, rallied me a good deal on my new acquaintance, and in the humour of her ideas I wrote some lines, which I enclose you, as I think they have a good deal of poetic merit ; and Miss Nimmo tells me you are not only a critic but a poetess. Fiction, you know, is the native region of poetry ; and I hope you will pardon my vanity in sending you the *bagatelle* as a tolerable off-hand *jeu-d'esprit*."

Clarinda replied, December 8, 1787 :—

"Your lines were truly poetical; give me all you can spare. Not one living has a higher relish for poetry than I have; and my reading everything of the kind makes me a tolerable judge. Ten years ago such lines from such a hand would have half turned my head. Perhaps you thought it might have done so even *yet*, and wisely premised that 'fiction was the native region of poetry.' Read the enclosed, which I scrawled just after reading yours. Be sincere, and own that, whatever merit it has, it has not a line resembling poetry."

Clarinda's lines in reply to those of Burns seem not to have been preserved.

In the fifth letter from Burns to Mrs M'Lehose, and the first letter in which the fair correspondent is described Clarinda by the poet, who signs himself Sylvander, he refers to a short letter, which has also been lost, accompanying some impromptu verses. In that letter the poet very probably explained the reason for using the Arcadian appellations; but it is just possible Mrs M'Lehose was the first to sign herself Clarinda, and that the poet followed suit by adopting Sylvander as his *nom de guerre*. On December 28, 1787, he writes :—

" I beg your pardon, my dear ' Clarinda,' for the fragment scrawl I sent you yesterday. I really don't know what I wrote."

" Yesterday " would be the 27th of December; but the letter from the poet immediately preceding the one from which our extract is made, is dated Thursday, 20th December.

Clarinda, writing under date January 3, 1788, says :—

" I got your lines: they are ' in *kind !*' I can't but laugh at my presumption in pretending to send my poor ones to *you !* but it was to amuse myself."

Here, again, remarks Mr W. Scott Douglas, the lines of Burns have been lost through some unaccountable remissness on the part of his correspondent. But, indeed, when scraps of the bard's handwriting grew invaluable, Clarinda became the prey of covetous collectors.

These notes may be appropriately brought to a conclusion by a few remarks on the misreadings of Burns's manuscripts to be noticed in collating the originals with the printed letters given in the Clarinda correspondence.

In the letter assigned to December 20, 1787, " I cannot positively say " has been misprinted

" I cannot possibly say " ; " something of honour" has been altered to "something like honour"; and "a vague infant idea" to "a faint idea "; while inverted commas have been inserted after, instead of before, " death," in " death without benefit of clergy."

In another letter, dated February 20, 1788, " concubinage " is represented by asterisks, and " hinted at " has been substituted for " insisted on." " Good things " should be in italics.

One other letter of the series, assigned to January 29, 1788, first printed by Stewart in 1802, should be dated at the top " Tuesday Morn," and " Love " should be substituted for " Clarinda " in the first line. The MS. is defective at the end, the last word being " hurry," as printed.

A Glimpse of Clarinda.

In Edinburgh "Sixty Years Since."

By James Adams, M.D., Glasgow.

(*From Glasgow Daily Mail, 17th August* 1895.)

Printed by permission of the Author.

> " Ah, did you once see Shelley plain,
>   And did he stop and speak to you,
> And did you speak to him again?
>   How strange it seems, and new."

"Oh yes, I knew the Duke of Wellington," said one of "the masses." "Well, we hadn't much talk ; for he was riding on horseback, and I was walking in the middle of the road, and—yes—he damned me to get out of the way. Oh, he was a big, brave man, and very easy in his manners."

By how many has it been regarded as a distinction or a memory worth recalling that he has shaken hands with O'Connell or Gladstone, hobnobbed with Pritchard the poisoner, or "rubbed shouthers wi' Burns." For he can say better than his neighbour whether they were tall, thin or squat, fair or dark, old or young, pleasant or grim of visage. Very trivial are such particulars, but they fill in lights or shadows of an otherwise imperfect sketch, which no mere portrait-painter's brush can give. Thus, I have never been able to see in my "mind's eye" the everyday aspect of Burns so well as through the presentment given in Sir Walter Scott's reminiscence of one meeting. And I never, without having my conception blurred, can look upon that commonplace map of Burns' features delineated in the cheap copies of the familiar Nasmyth portrait (not his full-length picture) which a loyal Burnsite has termed "that wishy-washy sheep-like face," but with a conviction that, if the striped vest with collar and coat with broad lapels were removed, and the face of any stout man of about twenty-eight years substituted, it would be a case of "take your choice." It is stated that Disraeli would not believe the oath of a man who could declare he preferred dry to sweet champagne; and I have similar disbelief of the person who professes to see in the frequent tea-tray portraits of Burns, the characteristic man, so instantly cognoscible in caricatures even of Napoleon, Gladstone, Bismarck, and such notabilities. "Burns' features," says Sir W. Scott, "are represented in Mr Nasmyth's picture, but to me it conveys the idea that they are diminished as if seen in perspective, . . . there was a strong expression of sense and shrewdness in all his lineaments. . . . The eye was large, and of a dark cast, which glowed (I say literally glowed) when he spoke with feeling or interest. I never saw such another eye in a human head, and he rewarded me with a look and a word, which, although of mere civility, I then received, and still recollect with very great pleasure." Such is Scott's record of the impression made on him, a lad of fifteen, when he met Burns in a company "where youngsters sate silent and listened."

Referring to Clarinda, it has been long known to some of my intimate friends that I passed an entire evening in a social party with that lady, when I was of sufficient age to observe, and they have often urged on me, as one of the very few surviving links between the era of

Burns and the present, that I should narrate
that experience, which, however trivial or plainly
told, cannot fail to be interesting, because re-
lating to an individual who occupied so much
of the thoughts and pen of Burns.　But so little
of a story have I to tell, that it is with
much misgiving I have yielded to persistent
insistence.

It chanced in Edinburgh (my birthplace) that,
when more than half-way through my "teens,"
and at the beginning of my medical curriculum,
I formed a temporary intimacy with a much
older fellow-student, who, beyond any individual
I have ever known, was stuffed with Scottish
songs, stories, and drolleries, as full as is a
linnet with melodious impulse.　He resided with
his parents at the Calton Hill, in a little by-
street which branched off to the left from the
east end of Waterloo Place, just where that
main thoroughfare reaches the Calton Hill.　My
friend invited me to a small evening party,
where he assured me I would have a "bellyful
of Scottish song," that being, as he knew, my
weakness.　It was no juvenile or dancing affair,
but a company of about a dozen middle-aged
individuals—decent tradesmen, with their wives

and other relatives—and I was the youngest person present. There was a supper, at which port and sherry in decanters were on the table, but scarcely touched ; and whisky toddy was served with the viands. Song, toast, sentiment, and story were the order of the evening, contributed by all in rotation under the option of drinking a glass of salt and water, placed in readiness, but on this occasion left untouched. There was present a chirpy old lady, who, from subsequent information, I know must have been about seventy-five years of age, but it was a considerable time afterwards I learned that in her an angel had entertained me unawares ; and that the " Mrs M'Lehose," with whom I shook hands and interchanged ordinary civilities during the evening, was the far-famed "Clarinda, mistress of the soul," of Burns. It was evident that she was an intimate friend, and highly regarded by the household. My friend, the son of our host, whispered to me early in the evening that she was a next-door neighbour, "a real game old lady," and an old sweetheart of Burns ; but he did not further enlighten me ; and at the moment I gave her little more consideration than I did others present, of all of whom I retain quite as vivid a recollection. The company was what many might consider very commonplace. Our host was a respectable master tailor ; one of the ladies a prosperous ladies' milliner—a fact impressed on me during a discussion on bonnets, then of a coal-scuttle shape, and made of Leghorn straw, both of which peculiarities, she confidently affirmed, would never be out of fashion ; a taciturn ship captain from Leith, with his sister, a lackadaisical, old-maidish damsel, bedecked with numerous thin corkscrew curls ; a hard-featured schoolmaster, or student's "grinder" in classics and mathematics; a coarse-mannered, boisterous master baker ; while a few others, more vaguely recollected, made up the company. To many the songs now before my retrospection may be familiar, but to me the musical part of the proceedings was most gratifying, some of the songs being heard by me for the first time. Indeed, I have a much more perfect recollection of the songs than of the conversation. The sentimental young lady sang " Alice Gray," and the " Meeting of the Waters "; her brother, " The Carse o' Gowrie "; the baker, " The Auld Man's Mear's Deid," and " The Haughs of Cromdale," both of which he gave with a "birr" and intensity of feeling that seemed to thrill him to the soul. The schoolmaster sang "Tak' your auld Cloak about ye," and "O Nanny, wilt thou gang wi' me," with a sweetness, tenderness, and humour that irradiated his countenance and showed how little one's outer aspect may correspond with the inner nature. Indeed, often as I have heard these songs, I have never since been so impressed, and all the more because his outer man seemed so rigidly severe. The ladies' milliner, a jolly-featured stout lady, with a deep contralto voice, excited our admiring merriment by the petulant girlish manner in which she sang "I won't be a Nun," which begins, I think—

"Now is it not a pity, such a pretty girl as I
   Should be sent into a Nunnery, to pine away and die ;
   But I won't be a Nun—I shan't be a Nun," &c. &c.

The plaudits she elicited would in a concert-room have meant a determined encore, and therefore with little pause she gave us, in great contrast, a very pathetic rendering of "Her eyes with her pale hands are shaded." I was much taken aback for the moment when she concluded and (with scarce an interval) abruptly called upon me for a song, for it was a privilege of the last singer to have " the call " for the next. I, however, gave, and doubtless in my very best style *con amore con spirito*, my pet song, " She says she lo'es me best of a' " ; and I have often regretted I did not take note of Clarinda's face as she listened to almost the only song of Burns' that was sung that evening. A fount of memories must surely have been opened. Of two songs, one a solo, the other a chorus, I have a very special recollection, as they were both heard by me for the first time— indeed of the latter I should say, the only time, although I have since been told that it is well enough known. These two songs brought Mrs M'Lehose conspicuously under my observation. The solo was contributed by my student-friend, evidently a favourite with Clarinda, who seemed to relish his pawky drolleries and broad humour much more than the ambitious efforts of some others of the company.

And here I have found myself almost uncon- sciously, or rather unavoidably, drifted into details of this to me very memorable evening, because they illustrate, and were in some respects

characteristic of, middle-class social gatherings
of the Edinburgh of that day, or "sixty years
since." There was no "wet blanket" in the
company to damp the current of song, recitation,
toast, and anecdote, which, with little inter-
mission, incited animated conversation. Indeed,
I never formed one of a group of more keenly
appreciative listeners and commentators. The
solo to which I refer was "My Wife has ta'en
the Gee," and the boyish Lord-Rosebery cast
of my friend's countenance as he enacted the
henpecked husband deprecating the sulks of his
wife, contrasted so much with his enactment of
a married man that the effect was irresistibly
ludicrous. The merriment became contagious,
and the company was convulsed with sympa-
thetic laughter. Clarinda in particular went off
into frequent "kinks," ejaculating now and
again, "Oh, stop him! take him away! put him
out!" while he perforce made occasional pauses,
gravely resuming as an interval of quiet per-
mitted. When he finished, she declared, while
breathlessly panting and wiping her eyes, that
"she did not know what he deserved for causing
her to make such an object of herself." I re-
member being strongly impressed with the old

lady's vivacious manner and lively spirits, so rare in one of her advanced years.

As " the night drave on wi' sangs and clatter," and toasts were being drunk, the ladies approving by sipping modestly at their small glasses duly kept charged from big " rummers " by the beau selected by each lady for that duty, the gentlemen showed their disposition to " let the toast pass " as " an excuse for the glass," by occasionally crying " clean caup out," and demonstrating by turning their glass upside down that it had been fairly emptied. Mrs M'Lehose, although she did not contribute solos, joined in the choruses with the youngest, and took her turn in proposing toasts and sentiments. These were varied, being personal, general, and some more homely than polished, as " May ne'er waur be amang us," " Our noble selves," " Thumpin' luck and fat weans," &c. Clarinda's first toast tickled very much our sense of humour. Looking round on the expectant company to be assured that all were charged, she proposed in impressive tone, " Our foes "—carrying her glass to her lips, but pausing as if from an afterthought while the company waited in puzzled suspense, she sharply added, " Short shoes and

corny toes," and took off her glass with a smack.
This, of course, was rapturously applauded, and
her health drunk " clean caup out."   One of the
chorus songs, which included " Blythe, blythe,
and merry are we," I heard, or rather saw, *per-
formed* for the first and, indeed, only time, al-
though it is not so rare as I long supposed.
The company were called to their feet by him
who for the nonce acted as leader or " fugle-
man," viz., the baker aforesaid, and we were
instructed to follow and imitate him exactly.
He stepped a pace behind his chair, and chanted
a doggerel lilt with corresponding gestures—

> " A' your right hands in, an' a' your left hands out,
>   Gie yoursel's a skelp, an' turn ye round about.

CHORUS—

An' hey for Ronald Macdonald, and ho for Ronald Macdhu,
An' hey for Ronald Macdonald ; we'll a' get roarin' fu' ! "

Whereupon all, with one hand elevated in front
and one extended behind, slapped our thighs,
wheeled and turned vigorously, coming back to
precision, as soldiers do at "present arms."   Some-
times our fugleman directed " fore ends in " and
" back ends out," " noses in " and " lang tongues
out": the wheeling, singing, and skelping giving

us all an exhilarating variety from the monotony of a long sitting, equal to that of Sir Roger de Coverley, or other spirited country dance. Clarinda sang, postured, skelped, and wheeled as vigorously as the foremost, and clearly with as much enjoyable *abandon* as she could have done sixty years previously, when amid her school companions she danced " Here we go by jingo-ring, and round the merry ma-tanzie," or any other of the out-of-door sports of Scottish girls.

We are all but children of a larger growth, and man is ever the same in his modes of thought and incentives to action. The Modern, trained in " dancing - school deportment," who may be reading with disdainful smile my reminiscences of the free and easy habits I am describing of middle-class Edinburgh society sixty years since, must be reminded of the saying that if you "scratch the Russian you will find the Tartar "; that if you strip the toga from the man you will reveal the pinafore of the boy. These sayings are true at all times, and equally true that "a little nonsense now and then is relished by the wisest men." " Leave off," said a great man when caught at some boy-play, " leave off, for here comes a *fool*," that fool being a Court functionary of many titles.

And here I admit that I had many misgivings that in venturing to pen my "Glimpse of Clarinda," there was risk of making sport for the Philistines, and grating the teeth of those who can only contemplate Burns' heroines through roseate curtains of the poet's imagination, if I described her, the inspirer of "Sensibility, how charming," while engaged in a game of romps, where refinement, modish tinsel, and varnish seemed to have no place. But in contrasting the manners of Clarinda's bygone time with those of the present, I think there is little to be noted of material change save variation or "marking time," as soldiers do while actively moving but not advancing. There has been no real progress in refinement since her day. The usages of a hundred or a hundred and fifty years back of the best Scotch society, to which Burns had occasional access, he has indicated in a letter describing his visit to a country mansion, where he with other guests and the young ladies of the family played "high jinks" in the drawing-room, "flying at Bab at the Bowster" and other romping games till early in the morning. His intercourse with

male society—with the Crochallan Club in Edin-
burgh—the dining parties at country gentlemen's
houses (as illustrated in Sir W. Scott's "Guy
Mannering," wherein the frolics of Councillor
Pleydell with his brother lawyers in Edinburgh
are recorded), show that even the usages of
middle-class life in the Edinburgh of sixty years
ago compare not unfavourably with those of the
sister country then or now. "There is a deal of
human natur' about," we are told by that astute
philosopher, Sam Slick. In his "Experiences
of a Barrister's Life" (1882), Serjeant Ballantine
refers to his pupilage in the early part of the
present century, and tells us that in London,
"vice clothed in its most repulsive garb stalked
publicly through the streets; . . . there was an
atmosphere of coarseness and slang, and even in
private society toasts were given and conversa-
tion tolerated that would now shock the least
refined; . . . and songs of a degrading and
filthy character were sung. . . . Most of my
readers will remember a scene described by
Thackeray in his novel of 'The Newcomes,'
referring to this subject, which is far more
graphic and powerful than any I can attempt."
If we seek evidence in support of Serjeant

Ballantine's belief in a better state of present
things, what do we find? We need only look
at the current periodical press—whether of the
masses or classes is immaterial. I take up a
London weekly journal called *Modern Society*,
which professedly holds the mirror up to nature,
and has for its motto, "Society sayings and
doings"—the sayings and doings of one week
being nearly a repetition of the last, and that
the counterpart of the next. In an issue of July
1894, with reference to "Lady B——'s dance,"
the editor of *Society* remarks : "What a relief
it is to every one when there are few boys [*i.e.*,
young gentlemen]. . . . One of the most
objectionable habits of ' boydom ' of the present
day is the habit of gathering in groups at the
supper table, and relating stories which are only
fit for the smoking room, quite regardless of the
presence of ladies." Here this censor of a com-
munity that has a Royal Court for its centre,
suggests that habits and conversation that are
everywhere degrading and unfit for gentlemen
and ladies, are nevertheless to be tolerated if
reserved " for the smoking - room." *Quis cus-
todiet ipsos custodes?* See also the writings of
George Moore or Zola, characterised by the

Examiner as fit objects for being burned by the common hangman. Surely there is no need for me to excuse the revelry of that evening when I had my glimpse of Clarinda! In fancy, nevertheless, I hear whisperings of "Vulgar," "Indecorous," and similar murmurs.

But in modern social habits there is a poverty of resources in promoting hilarity, and much therefore to be said in extenuation of that spirit of "gamesomeness," or kindly sympathy, that links us in active movements on a broad and general basis where all can personally join. It is this impulse of "human natur'" that sets a crowd of students singing "Pour out the Rhine Wine," when mugs of small beer sparkle on the board. It is this which incites immense political assemblies of city aldermen, merchants, and members of Parliament, to hail with harmonious welcome the patrician features of a Gladstone, the far-from-jolly countenance of a Beaconsfield, or perky phiz of a Chamberlain, by joining in the festive hymn, "He's a jolly good fellow," Despite the anachronism of "fellow," I can recall having joined lustily in thus acclaiming a former hostess, a benevolent, smiling old lady, and sealing pledges of hearty goodwill, with " three times three and a tiger." I discriminate widely between such innocent demonstrations of social glee and that "fascination for the unclean," indicated by Serjeant Ballantine and the editor of *Modern Society*. Naturally the soul repeats to itself all that is beautiful, or all that seems so. A writer, reader, or conversationalist writes, reads, and speaks of what he *likes*—of what is to his taste. And there is undeniably a strain in the taste of some men and women which enjoys the idea of temptation and of evil pleasures, even while resolving and holding on by his or her own rectitude. As there was no sign of evil proclivity in the social party I have described, I do not look back with any apologetic feeling for myself or my company in recalling the cheap and cheery " high jinks " in which I participated some sixty years ago with Clarinda.

I have never been able to blend my reminiscence of Clarinda with the familiar silhouette, in which she is pleasingly depicted, at the age of about thirty years (as I guess), in "full voluptuous but not o'er-grown bulk," decked with graceful, gauzy head-dress. I saw her a shrunken old woman, about five feet one inch in height, her head surmounted with a toppling, stiff, bunchy

" mob " cap, reminding me of old Mother Shipton
and of the refrain of a lilt I often heard crooned
over by an old nursemaid to the tune of " High-
land Laddie "—

"O what shall I do for starch and blue
    For my high Caul Cap—for my high Caul Cap," &c.

It is true there are few of us who recognise
ourselves or our nearest friends in portraits taken
at five or ten years of age, when contrasted
with one some forty years thereafter.   In recent
numbers of the *Strand Magazine* I saw a series
of portraits of individuals portrayed from their
infancy up till the present day; and among
them such notables as Disraeli, Bismarck, Patti,
Bernhardt, &c., and surely contrasts could not
be more dissimilar or less cognoscible.   Of
Clarinda's lively vivacity and graceful manner
I have a very clear impression, because asso-
ciated with a large lace shawl that floated from
her shoulders and waved gracefully while she was
gyrating in the " Ronald Macdhu " chorus, in
singing which, notwithstanding the chorus, no
one got "roarin' fu'."

Little doubt it is because of some disillusion-
ising personal accompaniments—such as snuff-
taking, to which she was addicted—that I do

not participate in the extravagant laudation
bestowed by some on the Sylvander and
Clarinda correspondence; nor do I share the
feeling which some Burns critics evince in re-
viewing that relation, or their indiscriminating
apportionment of blame because of his conse-
cutive association with Highland Mary, Jean
Armour, and Clarinda. He could not marry
Mary, for his liaison with Jean was "the clash
of the haill country side," and as such, no
doubt, was well known to Mary. But he could
philander and flirt as "a free bachelor" amid
"the banks and braes and streams around the
Castle of Montgomery," for the ethics of humble
country life were not more exacting than those
of the so-called better classes. It is unprofitable
to speculate from the meagre, *verifiable* facts
known what kind of wife Highland Mary *would*
have proved, for we know scarce anything of
her but what Burns tells us, although we love to
believe his conception. We cannot, therefore,
speculate with regrets, inasmuch as "fell death's
untimely frost, that nipped his flow'r sae early,"
left Burns doubly a widower—by death from
Mary, while her own resolve had widowed him
from Jean.

It cannot be denied that Burns was sincere in his admiration for Clarinda, which even he could not find words to adequately express in almost daily efforts, during their few weeks (about ten) of epistolary correspondence, and the few— not numerous—personal meetings. Throughout their short association he lived a lifetime of poetically ardent conceptions, and during the last eight days he was, he tells us, "literally crazed." For when Burns fell in love, as he so frequently did, "he liked to put his strength to it," as the Irishman said when excusing himself for sleeping twenty-four hours at a stretch. But after eight days' absence from Clarinda's immediate association, he did not at any time seek its renewal; not, I believe, because of any revulsion of feeling, but because of the sight of his *truly loved* Jean Armour, and because of her protestations that he had been misinformed regarding her real sentiments towards him. The renewed meetings, and Jean's assurances, evoked the *real* passion which had perhaps slumbered, but had ever been cherished, for the woman who, till his latest hour, continued to be *his* "Jean." I doubt, indeed, if Burns, until this critical time, ever fully understood, or seriously analysed, the

nature of his regard for and his relations to-
wards Clarinda, in which there was so much
more of the intellectual than of the animal that
usually predominated in him, as we are assured
by his brother Gilbert. For no sooner was he
outside Edinburgh, and removed from Clarinda's
immediate presence—no sooner did he rejoin
the long and always cherished object of that
real passion—no sooner was he assured by his
Jean that, despite her forced renunciation, she
loved him as heretofore—no sooner did he learn
from her family that the obstacles previously
interposed were swept aside in view of his im-
proved fortunes and rising social position, than
he hastened to renew the broken link by a
second and more formal marriage under Church
sanction ; and thus he broke for ever from the
craze of "infirm resolves," which for some time
after his temporary estrangement from Jean
Armour had characterised his actions in relation
to her. He now saw clearly that the happiness
or misery of a much-loved and much-trusting
woman was in his hands—that immediate
decision was imperative, and some discredit
unavoidable, but least discredit to those he had
unwisely involved, if he accepted for himself the

larger share; and he then resolutely selected that path which duty and long-enduring affection alike indicated. And Clarinda was thereafter avoided by him, but she continued to be tenderly recollected, respected, and admired. "Had Burns deserted her (Jean Armour), he had merely been a heartless villain," says Professor Wilson. "In making her his lawful wedded wife, he did no more than any other man, deserving the name of man, in the same circumstances would have done; and had he not, he would have walked in shame before men, and in fear and trembling before God."

He reaped the reward of an honest resolve in his calm domestic hearth, and did the best that the circumstances allowed; and the best for, and by Clarinda; who, although in many respects "a charming woman," showed in her brief relations with Burns that "charming women are apt to have wills of their own"—a will with which that of the poet would assuredly have clashed, as it never did with that of his evenly-minded Jean. It should, therefore, be matter of congratulation that it was never of his much-loved respected wife, Jean Armour, but only of Clarinda, that Burns spoke when he referred to her as "a *ci-devant* goddess of mine," and to whom he wrote, " But, by heavens, madam, I will not be bullied." And those who lament the Sylvander and Clarinda correspondence may take comfort, despite the poetic " heart-wrung tears and warring sighs and groans," that all happened for the best ; and that the end fitly crowned the whole.

Some weeks after the meeting I have endeavoured to describe, and during which I had that glimpse of Clarinda which has aided my judgment of her character, I met casually the schoolmaster, and in the gossip that followed I learned much that made the evening more remarkable, and riveted on my memory some of the details. " Ay," he said, with a tenderly regretful smile as we parted, " it was indeed a sunny blink "—

> " It was but ae night o' our lives,
> And wha wad grudge though it were twa?"

The Real Clarinda.

By PETER ROSS, LL.D., Author of "The Scot in America," &c. &c.

———

THE loves of Burns are among the most interesting studies in the career of that most gifted of men. His love passages were so many, and had such an influence in shaping the events and fortunes of his life, that we must study them, patiently and thoroughly, to understand his character and much of the apparent weakness and carelessness which came over him at times ; and to discover how a being so wondrously endowed could exhibit so many peculiar inconsistencies in his mental make up. It is not going beyond the authentic facts which we have concerning that life of thirty-seven years, to say that it was mainly directed, controlled, and influenced, and to a very great extent inspired, by its love for the society of the sex opposite to its own. The peculiar thing about the love passages of Burns is that they all continued to preserve for him a niche in the hearts of those who won his

affections long after each reign was over, no matter
what changes afterward took place in their lives,
their conditions, their circumstances. Burns was
his mother's favourite as a boy, and until the
close of her long life he had the dearest place in
her heart. Jean Armour, in her years of widow-
hood, seemed only, as time sped on, to live in
the hope of being again united to him for whom
she had once sacrificed all, and who had raised
her, a peasant girl, to a place among the most
noted women of the world ; and Clarinda, with
the weight of eighty years of life—a life which
early was clouded with sorrow—remembered
keenly, yet affectionately, the incidents of her
love passage with the poet till the last.

The biographers and critics of Burns treat the
Clarinda love episode in a rather peculiar fashion.
Some of them barely mention it ; others do not
seem able to understand it exactly. Robert
Chambers, the best of them all, seemingly has
suspicions that it was very wrong, very indis-
creet altogether ; and gravely moralises con-
cerning it at intervals,—a course which was not
very usual with him. He does not exactly
assert that the love passage had any illicit
details ; he presents the case as fully as pos-

L

sible, and renders a verdict of not proven. Scott
Douglas, by implication rather than assertion,
would have us believe that the love was not
altogether innocent. Hately Waddell roundly
denounces " Clarinda," and says in effect that
" she was no better than she should be." Blackie
thinks the interlude perfectly innocent. Prin-
cipal Shairp does not discuss the nature of the
intimacy, but condemns the artificial style of
Burns's letters, and is disposed to frown upon the
woman.   Lockhart calls the passage "a little
romance." The others are more or less non-
committal, or unjust, or supercilious. The in-
cident has been treated in a really critical
fashion only by Chambers, and, as we have said,
he did not express an opinion with any definite-
ness either way. But he really sums up all that
can be said truthfully on the subject from the
point of one who believes in the existence of
something more than mere words. The other
side is stated, by one who evidently never con-
ceived that there was anything in the friend-
ship that was not in every way commendable, in
the little book on Clarinda issued in 1843 by her
grandson.

It is a significant fact, we think, that none of

Clarinda's friends believed that her relations with Burns were anything but what might be perfectly proper between a married woman on the one hand and a warm personal friend on the other. Edinburgh, at the time the episode took place, was little better than a big village, where the people revelled in gossip, where scandal was always a timely topic, and each morsel acquired new importance as it came from the lips of a new whisperer. If the relations between Burns and Clarinda had been such as to afford any room for doubt, or for ill-natured suspicion, something of it would undoubtedly have reached the ears of Clarinda's kinsman and benefactor, Lord Craig, one of the Judges of the Court of Session. But until his death, in 1813, that upright and amiable man continued to the lady his kindly protection, and never entertained any doubt as to the rectitude of her moral character, even although the extraordinary letters which passed between her and the poet had been printed and published several years before. Her personal friends seemed to have entertained no thought of there being anything unworthy in her friendship with the poet, and those who were acquainted with her at a later period of her life held her in too high esteem, and judged her character too noble and kindly, to permit them to imagine for a moment that she had ever exceeded the bounds of discretion even in her admiration for her country's bard.

That Clarinda truly loved Burns there seems no reason to doubt. Her own words, as we read them, impress that fact even on a casual reader. If we study her letters closely we can follow the progress of her sentiments through simple friendship, induced primarily for the poet who had won such extraordinary fame by the manner in which he had interpreted the hearts of his countrymen, until we find friendship develop into love, and then that love become so intense that it throws off all reserve and delights in acknowledgment. That Clarinda would have united her fortunes with those of the poet had the divorce machinery in the Scotch Courts been as easily worked then as now, seems reasonable to assume. But divorce was little thought of in Scotland in her day, and she could only bid him wait and hope, two qualities which seem to have been lacking in the poet's mental equipment. That she grieved when Burns by his open marriage with Jean Armour increased the barriers between them is certain ; that she then abandoned all hope of being to him any more than a casual friend is equally certain. But it is true, too, that she never gave up her love, that time only deepened the impression he had made on her heart, and that the 6th of each December was always a sad anniversary for her, as on that date, to quote her own words, written many, many years after, she " parted with Burns in the year 1791, never more to meet in this world," and she added to the record the touching words, " Oh, may we meet in heaven."

It is probable that in his whole career Burns met no woman who, to adapt the Duchess of Gordon's expression, carried him " off his feet " more completely than did Clarinda. This we say with full knowledge of the true wifely qualities of " Bonnie Jean," the mysterious passion for Highland Mary, and the undisguised admiration which the poet so freely expressed for others of the " darling sex " in all ranks of life. Chambers rightly gives the reason for this when he says : " Mrs M'Lehose was exactly the kind of woman to fascinate Burns. She might indeed be described as the town-bred or lady analogue of the country maidens who had exercised the greatest power over him in his earlier days." She had been unfortunate in her marriage, and moved in her own circle with the freedom which marriage, no matter how unfortunate, bestowed upon women. Her husband had deserted her; his conduct was little short of brutal; and she evidently had done nothing to merit her misfortunes or to be placed in the dubious position of a wife who had been abandoned by him to whom she had once given her heart, and who had sworn to protect her. Every one pitied her, no one had a word to say in defence of her husband, and as we read the entire history of the ill-assorted couple, now that the record is complete, we can regard him as nothing else than a base wretch, who passed through life, for some inscrutable reason, without receiving the punishment which his cruel and heartless conduct to his wife and children would have justified. Clarinda, in spite of the blandishments of the poet, and in spite, too, of her own evident infatuation, remained true to the vows she took upon herself when she became the wife of James M'Lehose until the end of her career. James M'Lehose, on the other hand, violated them all. He was regarded as a "respectable" man until the close of his ignoble life, in 1812. She was regarded soon after the publication of her correspondence with Burns with suspicion, and even till the present day the literary ghouls, who have tried to blacken the memory of "Scotia's darling poet," still affect to sneer at the conduct of a woman who in reality lived an honourable life, who devoted herself to her children, and whose almost last words were, "I go to Jesus." Surely, too, the ingenuity of evil conjecture might have spared the heroine who inspired that sweetest of songs, "My Nannie's Awa'."

Burns was not attracted to Clarinda solely by her misfortunes. She was a beautiful woman, accomplished beyond most women in her station of life, sprightly in her manners, agreeable in her conversation, and possessing considerable poetic ability as well as excellent literary taste. If we were to judge of her relations with Burns by the code of morals which is presumed to prevail in our day, were her letters and his to be presented as proofs of wrongdoing under present conditions, they might, we freely admit, give rise to conjecture. But we must remember they were written in a time when people were more outspoken than now, when manners were not so strait-laced, when people talked more freely concerning many matters than they now dare to think of them. We should also remember that Mrs M'Lehose, as a married woman, had no need of comporting herself with the reserve that would be natural in a spinster, that her disposition was inclined to be gay and happy, and her desire was to forget the sad position in which she was placed by her husband's selfish conduct. But, even before the Burns interlude in her career had reached much headway, she complained in a letter to the poet that the world regarded her natural inclination for gaiety with grave doubt. " In reading the account," she wrote, " you gave of your inveterate turn for social pleasures, I smiled at its resemblance to my own. It is so great that I often think I had been a man but for some mistake of nature. If you saw me in a merry party you would suppose me only an enthusiast in fun; but I now avoid parties. My spirits are sunk for days after; and what is worse, there are sometimes dull or malicious souls who censure me loudly for what their sluggish nature cannot comprehend."

While, doubtless, Clarinda's beauty and sprightliness had much to do with attracting the fancy of Burns, it was her accomplishments, her sentiments, that really threw him at her feet. Except in religion, her views generally were more like those entertained by the poet than, so far as we know, were held by any other woman of his acquaintance, no matter in what rank. She was at least equal to the poet in her ability to converse on philosophical, social, or abstruse questions, and her conversation seems seldom to have been commonplace. She could be frivolous, but never insipid; she could appreciate his varying moods; she knew enough of human nature to overlook his moral transgressions; she had the same profound contempt for cant that he had, the same lack of appreciation of rank for the sake of rank alone, the same ideas of human equality. There was nothing squeamish in her disposition. She met the poet on an equal footing, but never forgot, even when he held full possession of her heart, that there was a barrier between them which time alone had any chance of removing.

Such sentiments as those indicated in the following lines must have went directly to the heart of the poet as he read them in one of her impassioned letters: " A recontre to-day I will relate to you, because it will show you I have my own share of pride. I met with a sister of Lord Napier at the house of a friend with whom I sat between sermons. I knew who she was, but paid her no other marks of respect than I do to any gentlewoman. She eyed me with minute supercilious attention, never looking at me when I spoke, but even half interrupted me before I had done addressing the lady of the house. I felt my face glow with resentment, and consoled myself with the idea of being her superior in every respect but the accidental, trifling one of birth! I was disgusted at the fawning deference the lady showed her; and when she told me at the door that *it* was my Lord Napier's sister, I replied, 'Is *it*, indeed! by her ill-breeding I should have taken her for the daughter of some upstart tradesman.'" The following is another picture which, we may feel sure, impressed itself vividly on the imagination, as it undoubtedly must have fired the heart of the poet: "I'll tell you a pretty apt quotation I made to-day, warm from my heart. I met the Judges [Lords of Session] in the morning as I

went into the Parliament Square, among whom
was Lord Dreghorn in his new robes of purple.
He was my mother's cousin-german, the greatest
honour he ever could claim ; but used me in a
manner harsh beyond description at one of the
darkest periods of my chequered life. I looked
steadfastly at his sour face; his eye met mine.
I was a female, and therefore he stared; but
when he knew who it was he averted his eyes
suddenly. Instantaneously these lines darted
into my mind :—

> ' Would you the purple should your limbs adorn,
>   Go, wash the conscious blemish with a tear.' "

Judging Clarinda by all the facts known of
her career, she had three leading traits in her
character — love, duty, religion. That she
surrendered her early heart to him whose
name she bore through her matronhood and
old age seems clear enough. That when he
forsook her, and she had abandoned all idea of
ever again being to him anything but a memory,
she yearned for some one to cling to, to love,
is evident to any person who reads her letters.
In one of them she freely says : " For many
years have I sought for a male friend endowed
with sentiments like yours ; one who could love

me with tenderness, yet unmixed with selfish-
ness; who could be my friend, companion,
protector, and who would die sooner than
injure me." That she gave forth all the love
in her nature to the poet is also evident; every
one of her letters is sufficient testimony to that,
and also to the fact that her love developed and
strengthened as the days passed on, and the two
became more thoroughly acquainted with each
other's brilliant qualities. But duty forbade her
doing aught that might injure her fair reputation
or cause her children, as they grew up, a tinge
of shame. Her letters are invariably clear and
emphatic on this point. In an early epistle she
warns the poet: "I am your friend, Sylvander;
take care lest virtue demand even friendship as
a sacrifice." Toward the close of the episode
she wrote: "I believe our friendship will be
lasting; its basis has been similarity of tastes,
feelings, and sentiments;" and once she uttered
the key-note of her own position in these words:
"I laugh to myself at the recollection of your
earnest asseverations as to being anti-platonic.
Want of passions is not merit. Strong ones
under the control of reason and religion—let
these be our glory."

Her strong sense of duty, mingled with love, entered into all the other details of her life. To her children she was devoted, and her devotion was inspired not merely by maternal instinct, but also by an elevated view of her moral obligations and accountability. This is sufficiently shown by the following words: " I have slept little these two nights. My child was uneasy, and that kept me awake watching him. Sylvander, if I have merit in anything, 'tis in an unremitting attention to my two children ; but it cannot be denominated merit, since 'tis as much inclination as duty. A prudent woman (as the world goes) told me she was surprised I loved them, ' considering what a father they had.' I replied with acrimony, I could not but love my children in any case ; but my having given them the misfortune of such a father endears them doubly to my heart. They are innocent ; they depend on me, and I feel this the most tender of all claims. While I live, my fondest attention shall be theirs." On a later occasion, when she accepted her rascally husband's overtures, and accepted his proposal to join him in Jamaica (a proposal which he never dreamed would be accepted), it was a sense of what was right that influenced her decision, not inclination or returning love. To her kinsman, Lord Craig, she wrote on this subject: "I have done what you desired me—weighed coolly (as coolly as a subject so interesting would permit) all I have to suffer or expect in either situation, and the result is my going to Jamaica. This appears to me the preferable choice; it is surely the path of duty, and as such I may look for the blessing of God to attend my endeavours for happiness with him who was the husband of my choice and the father of my children."

But religion was the foundation of this woman's entire conduct, of her walk and conversation through life. She derived her fixed religious principles from the teachings of her mother—a clergyman's daughter—and in all the tribulations, humiliations, sorrows, and cares of her many years, she ever found in the application of these principles her firmest stay, her surest hope. Burns' want of fixed religious belief she deplored as the greatest of all imperfections, the one that could not be overlooked; and she lost no opportunity of making the poet think on "the theme of all themes," as some one has expressed it. His apparent disregard of or unconcern about spiritual matters she apparently could not forget or forgive, although she thought little, as did most women of her time, of his social excesses and his unconcealed lapses into immorality. Some of her letters, indeed, are mainly devoted to the discussion of this subject. "Ah, my friend," she once wrote, "religion converts our heaviest misfortunes into blessings." Again she defines the fixity of her own belief and the want of any fixity in the religious sentiments of Burns in the following clear-cut words: "In most points we seem to agree; only I found all my hopes of pardon and acceptance with Heaven upon the merits of Christ's atonement—whereas you do upon a good life. You think 'it helps weel, at least.' If anything we could do had been able to atone for the violation of God's Law, where was the need (I speak it with reverence) of such an astonishing Sacrifice? . . . Ah, my friend, 'tis pride that hinders us from embracing Jesus! We would be our own saviour, and scorn to be indebted even to the 'Son of the Most High.' But this is the only sure foundation of our hopes." Surely no one can say these words (and there are very many like them scattered through her letters) could be expressed by a " flirting grass widow," a woman who did not possess in her heart that consciousness of rectitude of conduct and life which is the best human safeguard of virtue and honour.

No one knew better than Clarinda did the weaknesses of her own character, and she was constantly on her guard lest these weaknesses might, in an unguarded moment, lead her from the ideal of womanly honesty which she had set up for herself. She was not unmindful of the danger of incurring censorious remarks, nor was she above the feminine dread of causing suspicion by misjudged incidents in her daily life ; but, fully conscious of her own perfect innocence in thought, word, or deed, she did not always shrink from occasion for giving rise to remark as perhaps she ought to have done, and therein lies all that is to be condemned by any unprejudiced mind, if any unprejudiced mind could condemn at all, in her relations with Robert Burns. Her love for him was real, but it was purely platonic, although she would during the time the incident lasted have hailed with pleasure any lawful means by which Burns might have changed the status of a friend for the dearer one of a husband. "If a confession of my warmest, tenderest friendship does not satisfy you, duty forbids Clarinda should do more," were the words she had written when the flame of love between them was at its brightest stage. So she had written at the beginning of the correspondence, and her sentiments continued the same until the end. She conceived the idea that Burns and she were made for one another; and as her hopes could not be accomplished on earth she cherished the wish, long after he had been laid at rest in auld St Michael's Churchyard, that she would meet with him once more in another and a brighter world, a world where sorrow and separation are unknown.

That Clarinda was a woman of superior intellect her correspondence sufficiently shows. Her letters, indeed, are brighter, more logical, and far more interesting than are those she received in exchange from the poet. They are natural, unpremeditated, and evidently the simple expressions of her heart's thoughts. Those of Burns, on the other hand, are so painfully artificial, so commonplace at one time, so

M

bombastic at another, and at all times so stilted in their style, so burdened with the effort to produce effect, that it is with difficulty we can keep the poet in our mind as we labour through them. It would seem as though he knew he was addressing a woman of superior intellect, and dropped his own natural self in an effort to present to her something particularly striking, something worthy of her exalted taste and sentiments—and failed. In his letters we find plenty of Sylvander, but very little of Robert Burns.

That the poet loved Clarinda we do not doubt. That, had she permitted, he would have exceeded the bounds of friendship and propriety is only too evident. That he tired of waiting is also true, and that his love changed to feelings simply of friendship may also be allowed as fully demonstrated. When he left Edinburgh the spell of Jean Armour was again cast round him, and in his marriage to her he did what has redounded more to his credit as a man than anything else in his brilliant life. That he also loved Jean Armour is beyond question, but he was fitful and capricious, and wavered in his devotion. At these times other

women charmed his heart. Some of them had
cause to "rue the day" they attracted the pass-
ing attention of the gay, dark-eyed, lady-killing
young farmer-poet, or filled a temporary void in
his roving and wayward heart. Such certainly,
from the evidence alone afforded by the letters,
would have been the fate of Clarinda had she
not been fortified and strengthened by the fixed
religious sentiments which sustained her in so
many trials, and by her elevated views of life
and duty.

A true wife, a warm-hearted friend, a good
mother, a sincere, humble Christian, a philan-
thropic spirit, a creature of generous impulses,
Clarinda passed through her allotted years with
hosts of friends who loved, honoured, and in the
end revered her. Her life was wrecked almost
when she entered upon its pleasures; she had to
dree a terrible, a weary weird; but she never
faltered or lost heart, even when the darkness
gathered around her the deepest and the sea
of fate moaned the most hopelessly. Who can
blame her for valuing the friendship of that most
lion-hearted yet most tender-hearted of poets, or
censure her for, under the circumstances, freely
acknowledging that her heart was his?

And that was all. Everything seems to prove it, and the only detraction to her fair character comes from the surmises, the "ifs," the doubts, the contemptible insinuations and suspicions of a few literary vampires, who try to win notoriety or attention by their wanton liberties with the reputations of the dead.

A Tribute.

By Prof. JOHN STUART BLACKIE.

AT the house of an Edinburgh lady, Miss Nimmo, Burns had been introduced to a lady named M'Lehose, who being a spinner of verses herself, and of warm human sympathies, had naturally formed a desire to make a more intimate acquaintance with the acknowledged greatest master of the Scottish lyre. The meeting produced its natural result—a mutual recognition of social and intellectual kinship on both sides. The lady being of a frank and open character, and anxious to know something personally of such an extraordinary genius whom in his works she passionately admired, invited the poet to visit her at her lodgings a few days after the meeting. Burns agreed, and was to have taken tea with her in her lodgings on the evening of Saturday, 8th December; but the night before he was tumbled out of a cab by a drunken coachman, and got home painfully and with a severe bruise on his leg. The tea, of course, was suspended; but a lively correspondence was immediately set agoing, in which, from the high-flown and rapturous style of the poet, the lady had instant occasion to remind him that she was a married woman with a living husband, and he must address her only as a friend—the fact being that she had the misfortune, at the early age of eighteen, to have been united to a worthless husband, a Glasgow merchant, she residing in Edinburgh while he was holding his establishment in Jamaica.

But Burns was not a man to understand how friendship with a woman whom he greatly admired could be cultivated without passing into love; and so the lady forthwith found herself in the delicate position of being passionately admired by a man whose admiration she cordially returned, and that a man whose headlong impetuosity of temper was continually leading him to overstep those bounds which, in the intercourse of the sexes, are the shield of honour and the safeguard of innocence. Feeling herself in this situation, it might have seemed wise in a lady of religious principle and virtuous

habits—which Agnes M'Lehose essentially was
—to have shut the door after the first interview
with so perilous an acquaintance ; but her frank,
unconventional nature combined with her pro-
found respect for the poet to prevent this.
Besides, she felt herself firmly fenced with the
mail of a severe creed, and if she were able to
maintain her own position, as she did nobly,
she might also hope to use her moral influence
effectively in restraining the passions and guid-
ing the counsels of her admirer. The corre-
spondence of these two remarkable persons,
continued with little interruption for more than
three months, is in the highest degree interest-
ing, exhibiting perhaps even more strikingly, if
not more classically, than his love songs the
leading features in the character of this wonder-
ful genius. Love and religion certainly never
were so strangely tossed together as in those
impassioned epistles. In the following letter,
dated 21st December, after alluding to the
strong terms in which the poet had expressed
his admiration of her poetical talents, she goes
on to say: " Take care, many a ' glorious '
woman has been undone by having her head
turned. ' Know you !' I know you far better

than you do me. Like yourself, I am a bit of an enthusiast. In religion and friendship quite a bigot — perhaps I could be so in love too, but everything dear to me in heaven and earth forbids! This is my fixed principle, and the person who would dare to endeavour to remove it I would hold as my chief enemy. Like you, I am incapable of dissimulation; nor am I, as you suppose, unhappy. I have been unfortunate; but guilt alone could make me unhappy. Possessed of fine children—competence—fame— friends, kind and attentive—what a monster of ingratitude should I be in the eye of Heaven were I to style myself unhappy! True, I have met with scenes horrible to recollection—even at six years' distance; but adversity, my friend, is allowed to be the school of virtue. It oft confers that chastened softness which is unknown among the favourites of fortune! Even a mind possessed of natural sensibility, without this, never feels that exquisite pleasure which nature has annexed to our sympathetic sorrows. Religion, the only refuge of the unfortunate, has been my balm in every woe. Oh! could I make her appear to you as she has done to me! Instead of ridiculing her tenets, you would fall down and worship her very semblance wherever you found it."

Here, and in some other communications, she reveals herself as the most gracious and opportune of preachers. Calvinism from such sweet lips would sound quite differently than when thundered from the throat of the Rev. Dr Auld, of Mauchline, or any of his condemnatory brethren of the Evangelical type. From her elevated point of view, unsoiled by the mire through which her correspondent had sometimes dragged his eagle plumes, she saw clearly through his character, and interpreted the history of his religious experiences and moral aberrations, with that keenness and sureness of glance which belong to the moral superiority of the interpreter: — " One thing alone hurt me, though I regretted many—your avowal of being an enemy to Calvinism. I guessed it was so by some of your pieces, but the confirmation of it gave me a shock I could only have felt for one I was interested in. You will not wonder at this, when I inform you that I am a strict Calvinist, *one or two* dark tenets excepted, which I never meddle with. Like many others, you are so either from never having examined it with candour and impartiality, or from having unfortunately met with weak professors who did not understand it, and hypocritical ones who made it a cloak for their knavery. Both of these, I am aware, abound in country life; nor am I surprised at their having had this effect upon your more enlightened understanding. I fear your friend, the captain of the ship, was of no advantage to you in this and many other respects."

These earnest appeals and serious warnings of the good lady had the valuable effect of drawing from the poet his confession of faith in a more complete form than we find it in any other part of his works. A Calvinist certainly Burns was not; but though, like all emotional persons, repelled rather than attracted by the dogmas of a systematic theology, and though not infrequently seduced by his passions from his loyalty to his principles, he was by no means an irreligious man. . . . Our limited space forbids to enter more largely into these revelations from the inner soul of this man of large intelligence, noble aspirations, and ill-regulated passions. The more intimate relations with Mrs M'Lehose, or Clarinda, as she is poetically called, were abruptly broken off in March, when the poet left the metropolis for the scene of his early loves and rustic occupations in Ayrshire. . . .

In the month of February 1792, Mrs M'Lehose, after due consideration of a proposal of reunion on the part of her husband, set sail from Leith to join him in Jamaica; but she had not been long there before, from the continued unkindly conduct of her worthless mate, partly from the evil effects of the climate on her constitution, she was obliged to return to Edinburgh, where she lived and died at a ripe old age, beloved and respected by all who knew her.

All About Clarinda.

By ROBERT FORD, Author of "Thistledown," &c. &c.

(From the " People's Friend.")

To the question, " Who was Clarinda?" there are few persons of mature growth in Scotland who would not glibly answer, " Mrs M'Lehose." And further to this the most elementary and superficial student of Scottish poetical literature could tell that she formed a conspicuous figure among the dozen or more women who at one time or another made havoc of the heart of the National Poet. The full and particular account of the sadly chequered and interesting career of Clarinda, however, who, according to Burns' own written statement, had " wit and wisdom more murderously fascinating than the stiletto of the Sicilian bandit or the poisoned arrow of the savage African," is common knowledge only to the curious, who are the few. A brief sketch of the lady's career, together with a bird's-eye review of the Clarinda-Sylvander correspond-

ence, will therefore not be unwelcome here ; as
nought can ever be unwelcome to Scottish
readers which comes so near to the heart of
Robert Burns as to treat of one whose grace
and beauty and intellectual superiority evoked
his unqualified admiration—one who loved him
with her whole heart and soul, and was the
heroine of at least two of the most vivid and
tenderly passionate lyrics that came from his pen.
I mean " Ae Fond Kiss" and " My Nannie's
Awa' "—the former a parting song in which the
stanza occurs—

> " Had we never loved sae kindly,
> Had we never loved sae blindly,
> Never met—or never parted,
> We had ne'er been broken-hearted."

Making four lines of which Sir Walter Scott has
proudly remarked, " They contain the essence of
a thousand love tales."

Mrs M'Lehose, whose maiden name was
Agnes Craig, was no ordinary person, and had
no ordinary antecedents. She was grandniece
by her mother's side of the house of Colin
M'Laurin, the celebrated mathematician and
friend of Sir Isaac Newton ; and he was brother
of M'Laurin, the divine, at one time the minister

of Luss, on Lochlomondside, and latterly of St
David's parish in Glasgow, whose sermon,
"Glorying in the Cross of Christ," has been
described as the most eloquent in the English
language. The daughter of a Glasgow surgeon
named Craig—a gentleman also of good family,
which had its representatives on the judicial
bench as well as in the pulpit—she was born
here in April 1759—the same year, be it noted,
in which the song-celebrated "blast o' Jan'war'
win' blew han'sel in on Robin"—Miss Craig,
when only eight years old, had the misfortune
to lose her mother. But she grew and prospered
apace, and by the time she had reached her
fifteenth birthday she was regarded as one of
the beauties of the western capital, and had
received the distinctive and complimentary title
of "Pretty Miss Nancy."   In her sixteenth year
she was sent to an Edinburgh boarding-school
to complete her education. But previous to this
her beauty had attracted the attention of a Mr
James M'Lehose, a law agent in Glasgow. Up
to this time he had failed to obtain an introduc-
tion to her ; but on learning that she was going
to Edinburgh, he engaged all the seats on the
stage-coach except the one which he studiously

allowed to be taken for her. The opportunity
thus secured of ingratiating himself in the favour
of the handsome young damsel Mr M'Lehose
took the utmost pains to improve, and being pos-
sessed of an attractive person and most insinu-
ating manners, by the time their forty miles'
journey was completed he had made a very
favourable impression on the young lady's mind.
On her return to Glasgow, after an absence of
six months, he resumed his suit, and pretty Miss
Nancy Craig duly became Mrs M'Lehose in
July 1776, being then little more than seventeen
years old. The union was not a happy one, and
when two children had been born to them a
separation ensued.

"Only a short time had elapsed," said Mrs
M'Lehose, many years afterwards, "ere I per-
ceived, with inexpressible regret, that our dis-
positions, tempers, and sentiments were so
totally different as to banish all hopes of happi-
ness. Our disagreements rose to such a height,
and my husband's treatment was so cruel, that
it was thought advisable by my friends that a
separation should take place, which accordingly
followed in December 1780."

Shortly afterwards the husband, who seems to

have been in no way worthy of such an amiable and attractive wife, sailed for Jamaica in the West Indies, where he held latterly the post of chief clerk of the Court of Common Pleas, and died in March 1812.

After the separation, Mrs M'Lehose, with her two children, returned to her father's house, where she remained till his death, which event occurred two years subsequently. She then took up her permanent residence in Edinburgh, and lived in comfortable enough circumstances on the proceeds of a life annuity judiciously invested in her behalf by her deceased parent. Here, though comparatively a stranger, we are told, her youth, beauty, and exemplary conduct, together with the story of her domestic misfortunes, procured her many valuable and interesting friends.

In the closing months of the year 1787 the Scottish capital literally rang with the praises of the ploughman-poet. He was the local intellectual star of the period, and nightly claimed the admiration of all admirers. Everybody who was anybody was securing an introduction to him, and enjoying the luxury of an evening in his company in the house of one or other of the

literary savants of the city. By the good offices
of a mutual friend—Miss Nimmo—it was ar-
ranged that Mrs M'Lehose should meet the
poet. They accordingly met and spent an
agreeable evening together, just as the poet was
preparing to leave Edinburgh, and a mutual
esteem—perhaps we should say admiration—
instantly sprang up between them. A second
meeting was arranged ; but in the interval
Burns had an unlucky fall from a coach, which
so bruised one of his knees that when the even-
ing in question arrived he found himself unable
to leave his room. This circumstance delayed
his departure, and led to a correspondence—
which each of the two parties began by signing
the initials of their own names to their epistles—
and, after the first few letters had passed, con-
ducted as between " Sylvander" and " Clarinda,"
the first being the counterfeit signature of the
poet, and the latter that of his fair *innamorata.*
How much Burns was disappointed by not
being able to keep his tryst is shown by his
letter of the 8th December, wherein he wrote :
" I never met with a person in my life whom I
more anxiously wished to meet again than your-
self. To-night I was to have that very great

N

pleasure. I was intoxicated with the idea, and
if I don't see you again I shall not rest in my
grave for chagrin." Mrs M'Lehose's reply on
the same date is: "You shall *not* leave town
without seeing me, if I should come along with
good Miss Nimmo, and call for you. I am
determined to see you." As soon as Burns was
sufficiently recovered from his accident he visited
Clarinda at her own house, on Saturday, the 19th
January, and the result of the meeting was the
intensification of their mutual regard and es-
teem. Indeed, it was now the utter intoxication
of love between them, and the poet is ready to
exclaim, "Clarinda, first of your sex! if ever
I am the veriest wretch on earth to forget you!
if ever your lovely image is effaced from my
soul—

'May I be lost, no eye to weep my end,
And find no earth that's base enough to bury me.'"

The awkwardness of their relationship, it is
fair to state, was ever present to both. Clarinda
warns her admirer again and again that he is
corresponding with a married woman, and how
imperative it is for the fair reputation of both
that reason should govern all their words and

actions ; from affairs of the heart she bytimes endeavours to engage the poet in concerns of the soul, but they are both hopelessly entangled in the meshes of Love's subtle net, and only the enforced departure of Burns from Edinburgh in the middle of February could make them " tear themselves asunder."

They met only once afterwards, in 1791, but occasionally corresponded until within a short period of the poet's death, which occurred in July 1796.

Burns has been blamed by several of his biographers for his connection with Clarinda in the face of his previous engagement with Jean Armour, while others have contended that he was justified in believing that his engagement with Jean had come to an end. All we know with certainty is, that soon after his return to the country, his differences with Jean Armour and her family were speedily made up, and Jean and he forthwith became man and wife. So far as Burns was affected by it, the subsequent events fairly proved that the Sylvander-Clarinda affair was only for the moment rapturous, and once out of his sight, Clarinda was soon very much out of his mind. With the lady, however, it was markedly different. She loved the poet with a burning and imperishable love—a love which did not fade when she knew of his marriage with another—a love which did not cease when she heard of his death. In one of her warm, beautiful, and undoubtedly sincere letters we find her saying : " Never were there two hearts formed so exactly alike as ours. Oh, let the scenes of Nature remind you of Clarinda! In winter remember the dark shades of her fate ; in summer, the warmth of her friendship ; in autumn, her glowing wishes to bestow plenty on all ; and let spring animate you with hopes that your friend may yet surmount the wintry blasts of life, and revive to taste a springtime of happiness. At all events, Sylvander, the storms of life will quickly pass, and 'one unbounded spring encircle all.' Love there is not a crime. I charge you to meet me there. O God ! I must lay down my pen." In her private diary, written forty years after the date of her last interview with the poet, she has this entry :—" 6th December 1831,—This day I never can forget. Parted with Robert Burns in the year 1791, never more to meet in this world. Oh, may we meet in heaven ! " And Robert Chambers says : " I have heard Clarinda, at seventy-five, express the same hope to meet in another sphere the one heart that she had ever found herself able entirely to sympathise with, but which had been divided from her by such pitiless obstacles."

Subsequent to Burns' death, editor after editor of the poet's complete works—including Currie and Cunningham—endeavoured to get hold of the entire correspondence herein referred to, but Mrs M'Lehose, long and oft, with stern resolution, refused to deliver up her replies for publication. Allan Cunningham, when preparing the last volumes of his edition of Burns, penned the lady a long and earnest request, in which he said : " Without the letters of Clarinda, the Works of Burns will be incomplete. I wish to publish them at the beginning of the eighth volume, with a short introduction, in which their scope and aim will be characterised. You will oblige me and delight your country by giving permission for this. I will do it with all due tenderness. I have a high respect for your character and talents, and wish you to reflect that the world will in time have a full command over the letters, and that ruder hands than mine will likely deal with them." But still she would not be drawn, and many years had to elapse until the main bulk of the curious and interesting correspondence was laid bare to the public eye. Even now, it is only included in the more sumptuous and expensive of the recent editions of the poet's works, and in no single instance with so full an account of Clarinda and her relationship to Burns as is contained in this brief paper.

Mrs M'Lehose died in 1843, having survived Burns by the long period of forty-five years. In the poet's time she lived with her two children in a tenement-house in General's Entry, Edinburgh, the position of which is now occupied by one of the public schools of the city. It is due to her memory to state here that once at least in the course of her unfortunate grass-widowhood she evinced an inclination to rejoin her faithless husband, and with this purpose set sail with her children to Jamaica in the year 1792. On presenting herself there, however, Mr M'Lehose insisted upon her immediate return, on the ground that the climate would not agree with her, and she accordingly returned in the same ship that had taken her out. Latterly in Edinburgh she lived in rather humble circumstances in a small flat in a house in Greenside. In the last days of her life she never wearied of telling the story of her flirtation with Burns, and when showing to her cronies his faded love-letters, it has been said "she would just greet like a bairn."

Poor, loving, charming, trusting, witty, un-happy Clarinda! She loved not wisely, but too well.

Clarinda.

By Rev. J. C. HIGGINS, A.M., B.D.

AGNES CRAIG was come of good family. Only a few months younger than Burns, then twenty-eight, she was clever, cultured, good-looking, and possessed of no mean literary and poetic gifts. At their very first meeting there sprang up a strong mutual attraction. To her the poet wrote, "Of all God's creatures I ever could approach in the beaten way of friendship, you struck me with the deepest, the strongest, the most permanent impression," which warm avowal Mrs M'Lehose in reply as warmly reciprocated. The evening of that day on which he was thrown from the coach he had arranged to spend at her house; but being by his accident confined for a considerable time to his room, he began those remarkable communications which went on between them (sometimes at but a few hours' interval) for over three months. After a week or two they adopted towards each other the fanciful names Sylvander and Clarinda, and so they carried on a correspondence quite unique in the history of letter-writing. We further gather that after he was able to move about again, Burns paid Clarinda about a dozen visits before he left Edinburgh in the spring of 1788. Mrs M'Lehose lived until 1841, her eighty-third year, thus surviving Burns for forty-five years. After various ups and downs of fortune, she attained to better circumstances, and moved for many years in the best Edinburgh literary and social circles. Until her dying day she fondly cherished the memory of the poet—"that great genius," as she refers to him in her diary, under date 25th January 1813. Another entry, dated 6th December 1831, was found : "This day I can never forget. Parted with Burns in 1791, never more to meet in this world. May we meet in heaven!" Here we shall only add that, after a careful and candid study of this remarkable episode, we are able to believe that, though the position which Burns and Clarinda took up towards each other was, to say the least, a somewhat equivocal and dangerous one, it passed off free from actual moral stain. Clarinda's letters, being pervaded by an unquestionably earnest religious tone, drew from Burns sundry statements of his ideas on religion, of which we reproduce one passage in particular :—

"I am delighted, charming Clarinda, with your honest enthusiasm for religion. Those of either sex, but particularly the female, who are lukewarm in that most important of all things, 'O my soul, come not thou into their secrets!' I feel myself deeply interested in your good opinion, and will lay before you the outlines of my belief. He who is our Author and Preserver, and will one day be our Judge, must be (not for His sake in the way of duty, but from the native impulse of our hearts) the object of our reverential awe and grateful adoration. He is Almighty and All-bounteous, we are weak and dependent; hence prayer and every other sort of devotion. He is not willing that any should perish, but that all should come to everlasting life; otherwise He could not, in justice, condemn those who did not. A mind pervaded, actuated, and governed by purity, truth, and charity, though it does not *merit* heaven, yet is an absolute necessary pre-requisite, without which heaven can neither be obtained nor enjoyed; and by Divine promise, such a mind shall never fail of attaining 'everlasting life'; hence the impure, the deceiving, and the uncharitable extrude themselves from eternal bliss by their unfitness for enjoying it. The Supreme Being has put the immediate administration of all this, for wise and good ends known to Himself, into the hands of Jesus Christ—a great personage, whose relation to Him we cannot comprehend, but whose relation to us is a Guide and Saviour; and who, except for our own obstinacy and misconduct, will bring us all, through various ways, and by various means, to bliss at last. These are my tenets, my lovely friend, which, I think, cannot be well disputed. My creed is pretty nearly expressed in the last clause of Jamie Deas's grace, an honest weaver in Ayrshire: 'Lord, grant that we may lead a gude life! for a gude life mak's a gude end; at least it helps weel!'"

Side by side with his many rapturous outpourings to Clarinda, we find letters containing perhaps the most terrible expressions of unrest and self-upbraiding which even *he* ever penned.

On the 12th of December he wrote to Miss Chalmers :—

" I am here under the care of a surgeon, with a bruised limb extended on a cushion ; and the tints of my mind vying with the livid horror preceding a midnight thunderstorm. A drunken coachman was the cause of the first, and incomparably the lightest evil ; misfortune, bodily constitution, hell, and myself, have formed a ' quadruple alliance ' to guarantee the other."

Again a little later to the same lady :—

" Now for that wayward, unfortunate thing, myself. I have broke measures with Creech, and last week I wrote him a frosty, keen letter. He replied in terms of chastisement, and promised me upon his honour that I should have the account on Monday ; but this is Tuesday, and yet I have not heard a word from him. God have mercy on me ! a poor, damned, incautious, duped, unfortunate fool ! The sport, the miserable victim of rebellious pride, hypochondriac imagination, agonising sensibility, and bedlam passions ! I wish that I were dead, but I'm no like to die ! I had lately ' a hair-breadth 'scape in th' imminent deadly breach ' of love, too. Thank my stars, I got off heart-whole,

'waur fleyed than hurt.' I have this moment
got a hint. I fear I am something like undone,
but I hope for the best. Come, stubborn pride
and unshrinking resolution, accompany me
through this, to me, miserable world! You
must not desert me. Your friendship I think I
can count on, though I should date my letters
from a marching regiment. Early in life, and
all my life, I reckoned on a recruiting drum as
my forlorn hope. Seriously, though, life presents
me with but a melancholy path; but my limb
will soon be sound, and I shall struggle on."

And on the 21st January to Mrs Dunlop :—

"After six weeks' confinement, I am beginning
to walk across the room. They have been six
horrible weeks; anguish and low spirits made
me unfit to read, write, or think. I have a
hundred times wished that one could resign
life as an officer resigns a commission, for I
would not *take in* any poor ignorant wretch by
selling out. Lately I was a sixpenny private;
and, God knows, a miserable soldier enough;
now I march to the campaign a starving cadet :
a little more conspicuously wretched. I am
ashamed of all this; for though I do want
bravery for the welfare of life, I could wish, like

some other soldiers, to have as much fortitude or cunning as to dissemble or conceal my cowardice."

A comparison of these passages with the contemporaneous Clarinda correspondence once more shows, in strong light, what tumultuous fiery elements combined to make up the great, impassioned nature of the Immortal Bard—" So miserably open," as he himself has put it, "to the incursions of a mischievous, light-armed, well-mounted banditti, under the banners of imagination, whim, caprice, and passion."

A Brief Sketch.

By Principal SHAIRP.

JUST at the time when he met with his accident, he had made the acquaintance of a certain Mrs M'Lehose, and acquaintance all at once became a violent attachment on both sides. This lady had been deserted by her husband, who had gone to the West Indies, leaving her in poverty and obscurity to bring up two young boys as best she might. We are told that she was "of a somewhat voluptuous style of beauty, of lively and easy manners, of a poetical fabric of mind, with some wit, and not too high a degree of refinement or delicacy—exactly the kind of woman to fascinate Burns." Fascinated he certainly was. On the 30th of December he writes : "Almighty love still reigns and revels in my bosom, and I am at this moment ready to hang myself for a young Edinburgh widow, who has wit and wisdom more murderously fatal than the assassinating stiletto of the Sicilian bandit, or the poisoned arrow of the savage African." For several months his visits to her house were frequent, his letters unremitting. The sentimental correspondence which they began, in which Burns addresses her as Clarinda, assuming to himself the name of Sylvander, has been published separately, and became notorious. Though this correspondence may contain, as Lockhart says, " passages of deep and noble feeling, which no one but Burns could have penned," it cannot be denied that it contains many more of such fustian, such extravagant bombast, as Burns or any man beyond twenty might well have been ashamed to write. One could wish that for the poet's sake this correspondence had never been preserved. It is so humiliating to read this torrent of falsetto sentiment now, and to think that a man gifted like Burns should have poured it forth. How far his feelings towards Clarinda were sincere, or how far they were wrought up to amuse his vacancy by playing at love-making, it is hard to say. Blended with a profusion of forced compliments and unreal raptures, there are expressions in Burns' letters which one cannot but believe that he meant in earnest at the moment when he wrote them. Clarinda, it would seem, must have regarded Burns as a man wholly disengaged, and have looked forward to the possible removal of Mr M'Lehose, and with him of the obstacle of a union with Burns. How far he may have really shared the same hopes it is impossible to say. We only know that he used again and again language of deepest devotion, vowing to "love Clarinda to death, through death, and for ever."

While this correspondence between Sylvander and Clarinda was in its highest flight of rapture, Burns received, in January or February 1788, news from Mauchline which greatly agitated him. His renewed intercourse with Jean Armour had resulted in consequences which again stirred her father's indignation; this time so powerfully, that he turned his daughter to the door. Burns provided a shelter for her under the roof of a friend; but for a time he does not seem to have thought of doing more than this. Whether he regarded the original private marriage as entirely dissolved, and looked on himself as an unmarried man, does not quite appear.

O

Anyhow, he and Clarinda, who knew all that had passed with regard to Jean Armour, seem to have then thought that enough had been done for the seemingly discarded Mauchline damsel, and to have carried on their correspondence as rapturously as ever for fully another six weeks, until the 21st of March (1788). On that day Sylvander wrote to Clarinda a final letter, pledging himself to everlasting love, and following it by a copy of verses beginning—

" Fair empress of the poet's soul,"

presenting her at the same time with a pair of wine glasses as a parting gift.

On the 24th of March he turned his back on Edinburgh, and never returned to it for more than a day's visit.

Rev. Dr P. Hately Waddell's Views concerning Clarinda.

IT was on the occasion of his second visit to the capital, and some eight or nine months after the publication of his new edition, that his introduction took place, at her own solicitation, to Mrs M'Lehose, the celebrated Clarinda, a woman of genius by inheritance, and of fashion to a certain extent by birth and education ; whose misfortunes excited his sympathy, and admiration affected his heart ; who exercised upon him for the moment an exceptional but seductive power, more dangerous and discreditable to himself than anything that had yet occurred. In the lady herself there was frantic, hopeless passion, being still a wife, although practically widowed ; in Burns there was, to say the least of it, reprehensible acquiescence and collusion. All obstacles apart, he might have married Clarinda, of similar tastes, of similar constitution, and of the same age with himself—and would certainly have repented afterwards : as matters then irrevocably stood, he only dallied with her affections, and with her own deliberate acquiescence so far mocked her. To investigate this strange and questionable relationship would imply an analysis that must carry us far beyond herself; for the extraordinary moral problem presented to us by the competing claims of Mary Campbell, Jean Armour, and Mrs M'Lehose, for supreme domination in this man's soul within so short a period, is in fact the mystery that requires solution. It is as a matter of speculation, however, only, that it has engrossing interest now : for the death of the one, the repentance of the other, and the impossibility of success for the third, have solved it as a matter of history for us long ago. Mary Campbell, with her own rich freight of love and immortality, in the sea of hope, on the very poop of betrothal, sank and died—a loss that shall be gazetted for the world as that of an argosy ; Jean, the survivor of many a jeopardy and peril of her own creating, was acknowledged for wife at Mauchline, but with as little ostentation as possible,

having first had to brook her own shame ; and
Mrs M'Lehose, after the distraction of such a
desperate venture for the possession of such a
man, had to console herself that nothing worse
had befallen than her own inevitable disappoint-
ment. These are the matters of fact, and were
the final issues of the case, with pain, with
difficulty, and not without social damage to the
man himself, ultimately determined ; at which,
by-and-by for a moment, we shall hereafter
glance. But now, whilst his correspondence
with Clarinda, newly begun, still progresses,
and final separation, with seeming despair on
both sides, is not quite inevitable, the cor-
respondence itself, so remarkable in every way,
is what directly claims our attention.

That correspondence, the reader is probably
aware, was never an acknowledged literary
labour of Robert Burns—was conducted, in fact,
both by himself and the lady under fictitious
names ; and, for that reason alone, should never
have been intruded on the world as theirs.
Secrecy, and perhaps a sense of shame, were
connected with it. Towards the end of the
correspondence, which was long after he was a
married man, this is manifest—her very name,

according to his own explicit declaration, being still a mystery. It is not, however, to be regretted, in a psychological point of view, that such an extraordinary revelation has finally, even with indiscretion on the part of some, been authorised ; for it is in this correspondence that the very essence of his *imago* life, burnished like a sunbeam, but drenched in aconite, is really to be found. Beyond all mere fictitious imaginary love-correspondence in its vehemence, being prompted manifestly both by passion and by rivalry, and having conquest in both alike clearly in view, is this wonderful series of epistolary outpourings ; but distinguishable for ever from all genuine correspondence of love by the hardihood that flashes through every line. Through all imaginable disguises of Platonism, of theology, of moral respect, of sympathy, of deference, of friendship and concern for one another, the fever of eloquent expostulation and remonstrance and petulant entreaty rages, till both man and woman are overwhelmed and exhausted with their own theme. To be born of indubitable frenzy every hour, and maintained at its zenith for months, within the limits of propriety and reason, nay

with the solemnest recognitions of religion
itself, when appeals to the Deity were proper,
scarcely any extant correspondence of the kind
can be compared with the letters of Robert
Burns to this woman ; and the secret of this
is to be found unquestionably in the one source
of rivalry, as much as in the other of love.   His
letters to other women on the same theme,
and with the same object in view, might, no
doubt, have been equally eloquent and pas-
sionate, if other women had been able to reply ;
which they never were, except with bewildered
silence.   It was Clarinda's own faculty of re-
joinder that stimulated him to such efforts of
eloquence ; and his own love of victory, con-
joined with his belief in the possibility of
dissolving adamant with words, that carried
him ultimately beyond the veracities of his
nature in such a perilous encounter.   Alas !
for such unlicensed and seductive war.   For
his own credit and peace of mind it should have
been honestly abandoned when the inevitable
issue was foreseen ; and for her credit it should
never have been renewed.   But a man of his
stamp once harnessed for competition with a
woman, and furnished incessantly with artillery

by her own hand, was not likely to retire from the contest whilst a shaft in the quiver remained. For himself it was disastrous, and for her sorrowful. No good could come of it. There were ominous shadows of disgrace for him in such equivocal sunshine, and mischief for them both in such dread purgatorial kissings of the soul.

This absorbing, and it must again be admitted, most questionable relationship, seems to date from the beginning of December 1787— from the hour of their first introduction, in fact ; and may be traced by correspondence, with some slight interruptions and gradual diminution of enthusiasm on his part, till 1793 ; distinctly marked at its conclusion with anger, recrimination, and passionate regret. During the whole of the latter period misunderstanding prevails, for which the lady herself was unquestionably to blame ; and the correspondence of these years, apparently renewed by herself also, seems to be little more than a series of hopeless and fatiguing attempts to readjust a balance of respect for ever dislocated. But on a review of the whole, the difficulty to which we formerly adverted returns again—namely, how to explain the mystery of a threefold love during so long a period in one man's soul; for that Mary and Jean, the one in heaven and the other on earth, were still there is indisputable; and that Clarinda was there too, although with weakened sway, cannot be denied. The most exquisite lyrics to each of these three women are all to be found within this period— not fictitious poetry, but genuine effusions of the heart. All lower self-indulgence, disastrous and sorrowful, in which he sometimes compromised his own dignity for the delight of others, we omit to account for here: this alone—this triple waltzing of the soul, purely spiritual with one among the clouds; honest and affectionate with another on the cottage floor; questionable, but real, with a third through the post-office—with holy memories, with living love, with half-guilty fiction in the name of love—was indeed the great enigma of his life, and altogether inexplicable on any ordinary psychological principles. Could there be any serious delinquency, any practical moral disloyalty here? Difficult it would be to believe this; still more difficult with some not to believe it—for sin will be imputed by a few, where there is no sin, who cannot imagine such amorous extravagance as a normal condition of the soul. Be it so ; then David, Solomon, Sappho, and Petrarch were all in similar condemnation. He goes along with these in the biographies of the world, and was not unconscious of his own resemblance to the greatest of them during these very hours.

A Visit to Clarinda.

(*From " Old and New Edinburgh."*)

GENERAL'S ENTRY is, perhaps, now most intimately associated with one of Burns' heroines, Mrs M'Lehose, the romantic Clarinda of the notorious correspondence, in which the poet figured as Sylvander. He was introduced to her in the house of a Miss Nimmo, on the first floor of an old tenement on the north side of Alison Square. A little parlour, a bedroom, and kitchen, according to Chambers, constituted the accommodation of Mrs Agnes M'Lehose, "now the residence of two, if not three, families in the extreme of humble life." In December 1787, Burns met at a tea party this lady, then a married woman of great beauty, about his own age, and who, with her two children, had been deserted by a worthless husband. She had wit, could use her pen had read "Werther" and his sorrows, was sociable and flirty, and possessed a voluptuous loveliness, if we may judge by the silhouette of her in Scott Douglas's edition of the poet's works. She and Burns took a fancy to each other on the instant. She invited him to tea, but he offered a visit instead. An accident confined him for about a month to his room, and this led to the famous Clarinda and Sylvander correspondence. At about the fifth or sixth exchange of their letters she wrote : It is really curious, so much fun passing between two persons who saw each other only once." During the few months of his fascination for this fair one in General's Entry, Burns showed more of his real self, perhaps, than can be traced in other parts of his published correspondence. In his first letter to her after his marriage, he says, in reply to her sentimental reproaches : " When you call over the scenes that have passed between us, you will survey the conduct of an honest man struggling successfully with temptations the most powerful that ever beset humanity, and preserving untainted honour in situations where the severest virtue would have forgiven a fall." But had Clarinda been less accessible, she might have discovered eventually that much of the poet's warmth was fanciful and melo-dramatic. From their correspondence it would appear that she was in expectation of Burns visiting her again in Alison Square in 1788. She was the cousin-german of Lord Craig, who, at his death in York Place in 1813, left her an annuity, and thirty years after still found her living in Edinburgh. "She is now nearly eighty years of age, but enjoys excellent health," says Kay's editor in February 1837. "We found her sitting in the parlour, with some papers on the table. Her appearance at first betrayed a little of that languor and apathy which attend age and solitude; but the moment she comprehended the object of our visit, her countenance—which even yet re-tains the lineaments of what Clarinda may be supposed to have been—became animated and intelligent. 'That,' said she, rising up, and pointing to an engraving over the mantelpiece, 'is a likeness of my relative (Lord Craig), about whom you have been inquiring. He was the best friend I ever had.' After a little conversation about his lordship, she directed our attention to a picture of Burns by Horsburgh, after Taylor. 'You will know who that is ; it was presented to me by Constable & Co., for having simply declared what I know to be true—that the likeness was good.' We spoke of the correspondence between the poet and Clarinda, at which she smiled, and pleasantly remarked on the great change which lapse of so many years had produced in her personal appearance. Indeed, any observation respecting Burns seemed to afford her pleasure. Having prolonged our intrusion to the limits of courtesy, and conversed on various topics, we took leave of the venerable lady, highly gratified by the interview. To see and talk with one whose name is so indissolubly associated with the fame of Burns, and whose talents and virtues were so much esteemed by the bard—who has now (in 1837) been sleeping the sleep of death for upwards of forty years — may well give rise to feelings of no ordinary description. In youth Clarinda must have been about the middle size. 'Burns,' she said, 'if living, would have been about her own age, probably a few months older.'"

Clarinda in Old Age.

WHEN Burns revisited Edinburgh in 1787-88 he lodged with William Cruikshank, a teacher of the High School, in a house on the south-west corner of St James Square, in the New Town, and his was the topmost or attic window in the gable looking towards the General Post-Office in Waterloo Place. Herefrom Burns wrote: "I am certain I saw you, Clarinda; but you don't look to the proper story for a poet's lodgings—'where speculation roosted near the sky.' I could almost have thrown myself over for very vexation. Why don't you look higher? It has spoiled my peace for the day. To be so near my charming Clarinda —to miss her look when it was searching for me! . . . I am sure the soul is capable of disease, for mine has convulsed itself into an inflammatory fever."

The window of Burns was pointed out to an enthusiastic pilgrim, one summer morning in 1889, by an old resident of St James Square, to whom Clarinda had pointed it out herself. He remembered Clarinda (Mrs M'Lehose) in her old age, when she lived beneath his own father in a small flat at Greenside upon an insignificant annuity allowed her by her brother. She went once to her husband in Jamaica, but she did not leave the ship, as Mr M'Lehose insisted upon her immediate return on the ground that the climate would not agree with her. She was in very poor circumstances during her later years, but never wearied of telling the story of her flirtation with Burns. As the aged residenter remarked : " The auld donnert leddy body spoke o' her love for the poet jist like a bit hellicat lassie in her teens, and while exhibitin' to her cronies the faded letters from her Robbie she would just greet like a bairn. Puir auld creature, she never till the moment o' her death jaloused or dooted Robbie's professed love for her ; but, sir, you ken he was just makin' a fule o' her, as his letters amply show."

Mrs M'Lehose, deserted by her husband, lived in Burns' time with two young children in General's Entry, which lay between the Potterrow and Bristo Street ; but no houses dating back to Clarinda's day stand within a stone's-throw of Clarinda's flat.

The Original Portrait of Clarinda.

THE portrait of Clarinda, which Mr W. G. Roy, S.S.C., handed round for inspection at one of the Edinburgh Burns Club dinners, was the original picture which was specially drawn by the celebrated silhouettist, Miers, for Burns, and which was in the poet's possession at the time of his death. It latterly belonged to the late Mr James Gibson Craig, and was sold at the sale of his effects. It is now the property of Mr William Campbell of Cammo, and he has consented to its being preserved in the National Portrait Gallery, where it will be deposited through the Royal Scottish Academy. The presentation will take place shortly. The picture, which is in beautiful preservation, is very faithfully reproduced in Paterson's six-volume edition of the poet's works, edited by the late Mr Scott Douglas. The following are the letters which passed between Clarinda and the poet on the subject of the portrait :—

P

Thursday Noon, February 7, 1788.

" I shall go to-morrow forenoon to Miers alone. What size do you want it about? O Sylvander, if you wish my peace, let *friendship* be the word between us. I tremble at more."

Thursday Night, February 7, 1788.

" I thank you for going to Miers. Urge him, for necessity calls, to have it done by the middle of next week. Wednesday the latest day. I want it for a breast-pin to wear next my heart. I propose to keep sacred set times to wander in the woods and wilds for meditation on you. Then, and only then, your lovely image shall be produced to the day, with a reverence akin to devotion."

Clarinda and Sylvander.

By Alexander Smith.

THIS lady, who was possessed of no common beauty and intelligence, had been deserted by her husband, and was bringing up her children in somewhat narrow circumstances. They met at tea in the house of a common friend, and were pleased with each other's conversation. The second night after Burns was to have drunk tea by invitation at the house of Mrs M'Lehose, but having been upset the previous evening by a drunken coachman, and brought home with a knee severely bruised, he was obliged to forego that pleasure. He wrote the lady, giving the details of the accident, and expressing regret that he was unable to leave his room. The lady, who was of a temperament generous and impulsive, replied at once, giving utterance to *her* regret, and making Burns a formal proffer of her sympathy and friendship.

Burns was enraptured, and returned an answer after the following fashion: "I stretch a point, indeed, my dearest Madam, when I answer your card on the rack of my present agony. Your friendship, Madam! By heavens! I was never proud before. . . . I swear solemnly (in all the terror of my former oath) to remember you in all the pride and warmth of friendship until—I cease to be! To-morrow, and every day till I see you, you shall hear from me. Farewell! May you enjoy a better night's repose than I am likely to have." The correspondence so rapturously opened, proceeded quite as rapturously. It was arranged that in the future Burns should sign himself *Sylvander*, and the lady *Clarinda*. Each day gave rise to its epistle. Poems were interchanged. Sighs were wafted from St James Square to the Potterrow. Clarinda was a "gloriously amiable, fine woman," and Sylvander was her "devoted slave." Clarinda chid Sylvander tenderly for the warmth of his expressions. Sylvander was thrown into despair by the rebuke, but protested that he was not to blame. Who could behold her superior charms, her fine intelligence, and not love? Who could love and be silent?

Clarinda had strong Calvinistic leanings, and Sylvander, who could not pardon these things in Ayrshire clergymen, and was accustomed to call them by quite other names, was "delighted by her honest enthusiasm for religion." Clarinda was to be passing on a certain day through the Square in which Sylvander lived, and promised to favour him with a nod should she be so fortunate as to see him at his window, and wrote sorrowing, the day after, that she had been unable to discover his window. Sylvander was inconsolable. Not able to discover his window! He could almost have thrown himself over it for very vexation. His peace is spoiled for the day. He is sure the soul is capable of disease, for his has convulsed itself into an inflammatory fever, and so on. During this period of letter writing, Burns and Mrs M'Lehose had met several times in her own house, and on these occasions he had opportunities of making her aware of his dismal prospects. The results of his renewed intercourse with Jean on his return to Ayrshire were now becoming apparent. This was communicated to her along with other matters, and Mrs M'Lehose was all forgiveness, tempered with rebuke, and a desire for a more Calvinistic way of thinking on his part on religious subjects. That the affection of Burns for the lady was rooted in anything deeper than fancy, and a natural delight in intelligence and a pleasing manner, may be doubted. His *Clarinda* letters are artificial, and one suspects the rhetorician in the swelling sentences and the exaggerated sentiment. With regard to Mrs M'Lehose there can be no mistake. Her letters are far superior to Burns', being simple, natural, and with a pathetic cadence in some portions which has not yet lost the power to affect. She loved Burns, and hoped, if he would but wait till existing ties were broken, to be united to him. But Burns could not wait, the correspondence drooped, and a year saw all passion

> " die away,
> And fade into the light of common day "—

the common day of Jean Armour, Ellisland, and the Excise.

How I Lost the Opportunity of Meeting Burns' Clarinda.

By Thomas C. Latto.

ONE balmy afternoon in 1841 I was sauntering along the western slope of Calton Hill, Edinburgh, with my old friend Captain Charles Gray, lately retired from an active service of six and thirty years in the Royal Marine Corps, a poet himself, and one of the most enthusiastic admirers of Robert Burns that the Ayrshire ploughman ever had. The Captain, in his somewhat halting manner, for he had an impediment in his speech like Charles Lamb and Leigh Hunt, was never tired of discussing Robbie and his songs. Indeed, they formed the warp and woof of his conversation. Everything connected with Burns was grist to his mill.

At that moment a lean, thin-cheeked, sallow-faced man passed us. "Ha!" said the Captain, "a Yankee I'll be bound. There are unco few Scotsmen of that type."

"Correctly diagnosed, Captain," was my reply; "a genuine down-easter beyond question, but you can never guess who he is. Why, that is a grandson of Burns' Clarinda, bearing the same name too, M'Lehose. He has been in town some months trying to get some business settled in the Court of Session. I see him in the Parliament House nearly every day."

"Indeed," rejoined my friend, "that is somewhat strange. I was just about to touch on that very subject. Do you see that white-gabled house in the Low Calton, glittering in the sunlight?"

"Yes; I had observed it."

"Well, within that house lives the far-famed Clarinda herself. I visited her last week, and found her lively as ever, still worshipping the great poet's memory, and by no means disinclined to joke on the superlative devotion evinced towards herself in days of yore by the impassioned Sylvander. I have met her several times at the house of Robert Chambers, where she kept up the liveliest of talk with David Vedder, the host, and myself, and was quite the belle of the party."

"But she must be much changed," I remarked,

"since the days when she proved so formidable a rival to Jeanie Armour."

"Oh! that of course. The features are now somewhat harsh and haggard, very different from the rather attractive silhouette hanging in her little parlour. I cannot promise that you would discern in her now any traces of her once remarkable grace and beauty, but her interesting talk would be ample compensation for loss of personal charm."

"How I wish that I could see her," was my eager reply.

"Nothing more easy. To-morrow, or say Saturday evening, if that would suit you better," said the Captain; "and I shall be delighted to accompany and introduce you. She knows something of you already, and will be pleased to have a chat with you."

But that Saturday's interview was fated never to come off. There are so many slips between the cup and the lip in this uncertain world, and one must not count on many opportunities of meeting when the party to be interviewed is turned of ninety.

On Friday I read in the newspapers the announcement of her death.

A week or two afterwards I attended with the Captain a sale in Hanover Street, at the Auction Mart of C. B. Tait & Co., where the precious letters of Sylvander to Clarinda, preserved by her with loving care for half a century, were, by order of the grandson, her heir, disposed of to the highest bidder. To me it seemed like desecration to stand and witness these inflated effusions of genius at its worst, enriched, however, with various verses that had years ago "taken arles of immortality," dispersed in so summary a style. "Ae Fond Kiss and then we Sever," "My Nanny O," Agnes M'Lehose being the heroine of both lyrics, "The Queen o' Scots in Prison," going, going, gone for the few shillings that they would fetch. Alas for the poor widow's love-letters!

It may scarcely be worth while remarking that the casket in which the poor old lady had for so many years locked up these jealously guarded literary treasures was an oblong box about the length and depth of a fiddle-case, rounded on top, covered completely with a cheap, clay-coloured wall-paper, such as servant girls were wont to use in packing up their odds and ends when at Martinmas term contemplating migration from one farm - house to another. Such a "kist" as the sweet and guileless damsel portrayed by Willie Laidlaw in his delicious, imperishable song, "Lucy's Flittin'," represents as the receptacle in which the fair lassie rowed up her claes, not forgetting the bonnie blue ribbon that Jamie had given her for a keepsake and pledge of unchanging affection.

Some years after the worthy Captain's lamented death I scribbled off the following doggerel sonnet, which recently turned up in overhauling my memorabilia.

BURNS' CLARINDA.

As on the western slope of Calton Hill
Old Captain Gray and I had climbed the stair,
"See!" said the veteran, "yon white cottage; there
Clarinda, Burns's goddess, lingers still;
Still is she proud of that long-vanished time,
When the great bard would to her bower repair,
Fleech for a kiss from lips so ripe and rare,
And read her samples of his new-made rhyme."
"Oh, could I see her!" was my muttered thought.
"Why, yes, my boy—in very deed you may;
She'll like it; for she smiled o'er what you wrote:
To-morrow morning, or, say Saturday."
But many a slip I've found this one beside;
We never met—on Friday eve she died.

Burns and Clarinda.

By the Rev. ARTHUR JOHN LOCKHART.

I.

SHE was sae bricht, she was sae fair,
  She was of a' the warl' sae dear,
How could I choose but linger there,
  Wi' trancèd e'e, an' charmèd ear!
This is luve's morning-tide o' bliss,
  Wi' mony a meeting, heart to heart;
But, oh! luve's anguish, it is this—
  To kiss ance mair, an' then depart!

She was sae bricht, she was sae braw,
  Wi' sic a grace her charms she bore,
How could I bear to turn awa'
  An' look upon her face nae more!
Ah, we, wha did sae blindly luve!
  Felt we nae madness in the thrill?
Our dream is o'er,—yet, while we wove
  The flowery band, we dream'd nae ill.

She was sae bricht, she was sae fair!
  Now she ayont the sea is gane,
How can I seek the banks of Ayr,
  An' dwell wi' musin' thocht alane!
What solitude in ilka street!
  How gloomy seems each ancient pile,
Since fortune yields me not the licht,
  The gladness, o' her perfect smile!

She was sae bricht, she was sae fair!
  Ah, how will haunted Doon appear,
When simmer sweetens a' the air,
  An' a' her birds are singin' clear?
There must I sit me doun to sigh,
  As bitter memory comes again,
While the heart's ghaists gae flittin' by,
  An' a' the past is changed to pain.

She was sae bricht, she was sae fair!
  Her kiss was sweeter than the wine:
Now spare, ye win's, thou ocean, spare,
  The lovely form I dreamed was mine.
'Neath ither stars, on ither shores,
  When she has crossed the ragin' sea,
Ah, will the ane my soul adores
  Gie whiles a passin' thocht to me?

She was sae bricht, she was sae fair,
   And, oh, we lo'ed each ither weel!
My easy heart I'll blame nae mair,
   To lo'e her not it wad be steel.
Dear city o' my early fame,
   An' my ill-fated luve, adieu!
I seek the fields whence erst I came,
   To toil, an' weep, an' dream o' you.

II.

AH, MUST WE SEVER?

AH, must we sever,
   Dearest, for ever,
After the days we together have known?
   Yet, let me yet bless thee,
   Clasp and caress thee,
Ere thou wilt leave me to sorrow alone!

   Soft be thy pillow,
   Far on the billow;
Bright be thy dreams while thou speedest away!
   Every wave charm thee,
   Never one harm thee,
Cause thee commotion, or work thee delay.

Others shall greet thee,
Claim and entreat thee,
Yield thee affection, and make thee a home :
Thou may'st not ponder,
Hearts truer and fonder,
When dreams of the past o'er thy spirit may come.

Ah ! should aught grieve thee,
Wrong thee, deceive thee,
When we asunder for ever are torn,
Think of me, parted,
Sunk, and sad-hearted,—
Oh, but *thou* knowest how deeply I mourn !

Let one thought move thee,—
Still do I love thee !
Think me not cold who am only distress'd :
Come, if aught harm thee,
Shake or alarm thee,—
Fly like a bird to this sheltering breast !

Yet, why this yearning
For thy returning
Back to my arms, from that southern shore !
Passion beseeches,
While my heart teaches
That I, who have loved, shall behold thee no
more.

I have aspired,
Dared and desired,—
I have not striven for laurels in vain :
Song cometh, welling
From my heart, telling
All the sweet tale of our passionate pain.

I took Scotia's lyre
And lifted it higher ;
Thou art its theme, and its glory shalt see.
Past is its prime, now,
Brief is its time, now,—
Hush'd its wild music for ever will be.

Here must we sever,
Now, and for ever !
Sweet are the joys we together have known ;
But, with the morrow,
All shall be sorrow,
Thou wilt be absent, and I shall be gone.

The Poet's Immortal Wreath for Clarinda.

SYLVANDER'S REPLY TO CLARINDA.

WHEN dear Clarinda, matchless fair,
    First struck Sylvander's raptured view,
He gazed, he listened to despair,
    Alas! 'twas all he dared to do.

Love, from Clarinda's heavenly eyes,
    Transfixed his bosom thro' and thro';
But still in Friendship's guarded guise,
    For more the demon feared to do.

That heart, already more than lost,
    The imp beleaguer'd all perdue;
For frowning Honour kept his post,
    To meet that frown he shrunk to do.

His pangs the Bard refused to own,
    Tho' half he wished Clarinda knew;
But Anguish wrung th' unweeting groan—
    Who blames what frantic Pain must do?

Q

That heart, where mostly follies blend,
  Was sternly still to Honour true :
To prove Clarinda's fondest friend
  Was what a lover sure might do.

The Muse his ready quill employed,
  No dearer bliss he could pursue ;
That bliss Clarinda cold denied,—
  " Send word by Charles how you do ! "

The chill behest disarmed his Muse,
  Till Passion all impatient grew :
He wrote, and hinted for excuse,
  " 'Twas 'cause he'd nothing else to do."

But by those hopes I have above !
  And by those faults I dearly rue !
The deed, the boldest mark of love—
  For thee that deed I dare to do !

O could the Fates but name the price
  Would bless me with your charms and you!
With frantic joy I'd pay it thrice,
  If human art and power could do !

Then take, Clarinda, friendship's hand,
  (Friendship, at least, I may avow ;)
And lay no more your chill command,
  I'll write, whatever I've to do.

To Clarinda,

With a Present of a Pair of Drinking Glasses.

Fair Empress of the Poet's soul,
  And Queen of Poetesses ;
Clarinda, take this little boon,
  This humble pair of glasses !

And fill them high with generous juice,
  As generous as your mind;
And pledge me in the generous toast—
  " The whole of human kind ! "

" To those who love us ! "—second fill ;
  But not to those whom we love ;
Lest we love those who love not us !—
  A third—" To thee and me, love ! "

Clarinda.

Clarinda, mistress of my soul,
  The measur'd time is run !
The wretch beneath the dreary Pole,
  So marks his latest sun.

To what dark cave of frozen night
  Shall poor Sylvander hie ?
Depriv'd of thee, his life and light,
  The sun of all his joy.

We part,—but by these precious drops
   That fill thy lovely eyes !
No other light shall guide my steps
   Till thy bright beams arise.

She, the fair sun of all her sex,
   Has blest my glorious day ;
And shall a glimmering planet fix
   My worship to its ray ?

To Clarinda.

BEFORE I saw Clarinda's face
   My heart was blythe and gay,
Free as the wind, or feather'd race
   That hop from spray to spray.

But now dejected I appear,
   Clarinda proves unkind ;
I, sighing, drop the silent tear,
   But no relief can find.

In plaintive notes my tale rehearses
   When I the fair have found ;
On every tree appear my verses
   That to her praise resound.

But she, ungrateful, shuns my sight,
   My faithful love disdains,

My vows and tears her scorn excite,
　Another happy reigns.

Ah, though my looks betray,
　I envy your success,
Yet love to friendship shall give way—
　I cannot wish it less.

"I BURN, I BURN."

"I BURN, I burn, as when thro' ripen'd corn
By driving winds the crackling flames are borne,"
Now maddening, wild, I curse that fatal night ;
Now bless the hour which charm'd my guilty
　　sight.
In vain the laws their feeble force oppose :
Chain'd at his feet they groan, Love's vanquish'd
　　foes :
In vain religion meets my sinking eye ;
I dare not combat—but I turn and fly ;
Conscience in vain upbraids th' unhallow'd fire ;
Love grasps his scorpions—stifled they expire !
Reason drops headlong from his sacred throne,
Your dear idea reigns and reigns alone :
Each thought intoxicated homage yields,
And riots wanton in forbidden fields !

By all on high adoring mortals know !
By all the conscious villain fears below !
By your dear self !—the last great oath I swear ;
Nor life nor soul were ever half so dear !

AE FOND KISS.

AE fond kiss, and then we sever ;
Ae fareweel, and then for ever !
Deep in heart-wrung tears I'll pledge thee,
Warring sighs and groans I'll wage thee.
Who shall say that fortune grieves him,
While the Star of Hope she leaves him ?
Me, nae cheerfu' twinkle lights me ;
Dark despair around benights me.

I'll ne'er blame my partial fancy,
Naething could resist my Nancy ;
And to see her, was to love her ;
Love but her, and love for ever.
Had we never loved sae kindly,
Had we never loved sae blindly,
Never met or never parted,
We had ne'er been broken-hearted.

Fare thee weel, thou first and fairest !
Fare thee weel, thou best and dearest !

Thine be ilka joy and treasure,
Peace, enjoyment, love, and pleasure !
Ae fond kiss, and then we sever,
Ae fareweel, alas ! for ever !
Deep in heart-wrung tears I'll pledge thee,
Warring sighs and groans I'll wage thee.

THE DEAREST O' THE QUORUM.

O MAY, thy morn was ne'er so sweet
  As the mirk night o' December,
For sparkling was the rosy wine,
  And private was the chamber :
And dear was she I darena name,
  But I will aye remember.
      And dear, &c.

And here's to them that, like oursel',
  Can push about the jorum,
And here's to them that wish us weel,
  May a' that's guid watch o'er them ;
And here's to them we darena tell,
  The dearest of the quorum.
      And here's to, &c.

GLOOMY DECEMBER.

ANCE mair I hail thee, thou gloomy December!
   Ance mair I hail thee wi' sorrow and care ;
Sad was the parting thou makes me remember,
   Parting wi' Nancy, oh, ne'er to meet mair !
Fond lovers' parting is sweet painful pleasure,
   Hope beaming mild on the soft parting hour ;
But the dire feeling, oh, farewell for ever !
   Is anguish unmingled and agony pure.

Wild as the winter now tearing the forest,
   Till the last leaf o' the summer is flown ;
Such is the tempest has shaken my bosom,
   Since my last hope and last comfort is gone.
Still as I hail thee, thou gloomy December,
   Still shall I hail thee wi' sorrow and care ;
For sad was the parting thou makes me re-
      member,—
   Parting wi' Nancy, oh, ne'er to meet mair !

MY NANNIE'S AWA'.

Now in her green mantle blythe Nature arrays,
An' listens the lambkins that bleat o'er the
      braes,
While birds warble welcome in ilka green shaw ;
But to me it's delightless—my Nannie's awa'.

The snaw-drap an' primrose our woodlands
    adorn,
An' violets bathe in the weet o' the morn ;
They pain my sad bosom, sae sweetly they
    blaw,
They mind me o' Nannie—an' Nannie's awa'.

Thou lav'rock that springs frae the dews of the
    lawn,
The shepherd to warn o' the gray-breaking dawn,
An' thou mellow mavis that hails the night-fa',
Give over for pity—my Nannie's awa'.

Come, autumn, sae pensive, in yellow an' gray,
An' soothe me wi' tidings o' nature's decay ;
The dark, dreary winter, an' wild-driving snaw,
Alane can delight me—now Nannie's awa'.

MY LOVELY NANCY.

THINE am I, my faithful fair,
    Thine, my lovely Nancy ;
Every pulse along my veins,
    Every roving fancy.

To thy bosom lay my heart,
    There to throb and languish :
Though despair had wrung its core,
    That would heal its anguish.

R

Take away those rosy lips,
    Rich with balmy treasure :
Turn away thine eyes of love,
    Lest I die with pleasure.

What is life when wanting love?
    Night without a morning :
Love's the cloudless summer sun,
    Nature gay adorning.